DEA Intelligence Collection and Analytical Methods

R. Mammon

Foreword by

Col. D. Heller (Ret.)

CONTENTS

FOREWORD

Throughout my long career in criminal investigation, I have had the pleasure of working closely with Drug Enforcement agents on several occasions. They are the consummate professionals in their area of endeavor. At the invitation of the DEA, I attended several courses including a course on Intelligence Collection where this manual was among the training materials. Thanks to this type of cross training, our investigators increased their professional capabilities in both narcotics investigations and counter-terrorism.

Terms and nomenclature change over the years and since 9/11, some of the techniques used in this manual have new names. For instance, Agent Establishment is now termed Agent Validation almost universally throughout the Department of Justice. Computers using powerful software now give the analysts reach into the most shadowy secrets of criminal organizations. Despite these cosmetic changes and technological changes, the methodology presented in this manual remains sound and is utilized every day in the hunt for drug traffickers and terrorists worldwide.

COL. D. Heller, USAF (ret.)

1 ROLE AND CYCLE OF INTELLIGENCE

ROLE OF INTELLIGENCE

Reliable narcotics intelligence is the cornerstone of successful narcotics law enforcement. The large drug trafficking organizations have become highly sophisticated in protecting their operations, thus requiring a greater effort on the part of law enforcement to uncover the clandestine activities. The increased exchange of information among international police organizations has proven that cooperation, especially in the area of intelligence, is instrumental in combating large scale narcotics smuggling and distribution activities.

The Drug Enforcement Administration, Office of Intelligence was created on July 1, 1973 to assist in the collection, analysis and distribution of drug intelligence on national and International levels. DBA District, and selected foreign offices have intelligence units that supply narcotics intelligence information to appropriate law enforcement agencies both domestically and internationally. In addition, DEA has established the El Paso Intelligence Center (EPIC) which provides comprehensive intelligence support, particularly in the areas of air and vessel interdiction to appropriate agencies, EPIC is staffed by representatives from DEA, U.S. Customs, U.S. Coast Guard, Bureau of Alcohol, Tobacco & firearms, and INS.

Today, the Intelligence role and the meaning of Intelligence evokes varying opinions from military, government and law enforcement exparts. To some, intelligence can mean a select piece of information; describe a process of physical or mental acts; or define a specific area within a law enforcement agency. Therefore, the intelligence role is multifaceted and has to be understood or explained within specific areas. Generally, intelligence can be divided into four categories; knowledge, organization, activity, and product.

The knowledge category refers to information on hand or developed that gives insight into or identifies individuals/organizations and their activities.

This category of intelligence is the foundation upon which investigations are built and expanded.

The organization category refers to the unit within a department, bureau, agency, etc. whose function is to collect, analysis and disseminate intelligence information. (Example: DBA, Office of Intelligence.)

The activity category refers to the physical performance of collecting, analyzing and disseminating information.

The product category refers to the intelligence Information produced. This category of intelligence is the result of collection and analysis.

Historically, the roots of intelligence activity can be traced to biblical times when Moses sent several followers into the Land of Canaan for reconnaissance (numbers: Chapter 13, verses 3-5) . In addition, it is also known that Alexander the Great used an abbreviated form of the intelligence process to identify malcontents who had been destroying his army's moral. Later, in early American History, General George Washington provided information on enemy troop strength and movement throughout the American war of independence.
Most criminologists in the United States attribute the birth of the intelligence role in law enforcement to Det. Joseph Petrosino who commanded the New York City Police Department's Italian squad at the turn of the century. Petrosino was responsible for compiling and organizing extensive background files on numerous high-level criminals and criminal syndicates which had never previously been attempted. The information in those files lead to numerous arrests and convictions in the courts. Later, Det. Petrosino was murdered during an investigation
In Sicily, but his innovation left a lasting imprint. After his death, file research indicated that he and his team had verified all raw criminal data before documenting the facts thereby utilizing aspects of the intelligence cycle. Det. Petrosino 's success in combatting New York's criminal elements can be attributed to his belief in the value and application of the intelligence role.

Intelligence (ACTIVITY CATEGORY) is often confused with investigation and admittedly, a great many similarities exist. However, certain differences are noted. Specifically, investigative reports, sources, and methods of operation are usually available to a greater number of people by necessity than those of intelligence. In addition, arrests are made pursuant to our investigation, but are not appropriate to the intelligence collection phase. Lastly, investigation more often is reactive in nature and intelligence is usually proactive.
Earlier, it was explained that intelligence can be divided into four different categories by definition. In addition , two of the four categories (knowledge and product) can be divided into three different types. The three types of intelligence are as follows:

1) Strategic Intelligence

This is the purest form of intelligence. Strategic intelligence provides the law enforcement organization with an overview of criminal capabilities, vulnerabilities, trends and intentions with respect to certain specific areas (example: Heroin trafficking in New York City) .

This type of intelligence collection, analysis, and distribution allows law enforcement adequate time and information to formulate plans to combat criminal activity. The preparation of strategic intelligence requires the development of extensive knowledge of specific individuals, organizations and areas of criminal activity. This type of intelligence is developed over an extended period of time; one year or more.

2) Operational Intelligence

Operational intelligence, as the name implies, is geared toward and contributes to enforcement objectives. This type of intelligence provides data pertaining to specific individuals or trafficking organizations which have already been targeted for immobilization.

Information provided by this type of intelligence usually includes modus operandi, capabilities, vulnerabilities, sources of supply and trafficking routes utilized. This type of intelligence operation is normally of medium term duration; four to six months.

3) Tactical Intelligence

This type of intelligence is more oriented toward case prosecution than the other two types. It is targeted toward a specific criminal activity with the goal of neutralizing that activity. (Example: information received from an informant that a load of cocaine would be at a certain location at a certain time) Tactical intelligence is short term in nature, usually developed day by day.

The above provides an idea of the role and Importance of intelligence in the law enforcement field, especially in the area of narcotics investigations. It will be obvious, from the remainder of the manual, how the function of the intelligence process Is a key element In a modern strategy to combat the International drug traffic.

THE INTELLIGENCE CYCLE

The effectiveness of any law enforcement organization depends, in part, on its ability to obtain process and effectively utilize intelligence information. The ultimate objective of any law enforcement organization is to identify and immobilize criminals and criminal organizations. To that end, intelligence provides a service to enforcement by collecting, evaluating, collating, analyzing and then disseminating available information in the form of a finished intelligence product.

There are six basic steps involved in the gathering and processing of intelligence. These six steps are known as the Intelligence Cycle.

1) Collection:

The gathering of data or information which in its raw state or in a finished analytic report becomes intelligence input to law enforcement. Collection must be planned and focused to be effective.

It is impossible for any one person to know everything; however, it is possible for a person to know where to obtain knowledge or information on practically all subjects. The more sources of information a person has, the easier his work will be and the more valuable he will be to the organization.

Collection to be efficient must be focused. It must be directed against a target. The methods of collection utilized must be coordinated with respect to the target. A coordinated approach to investigating a given criminal activity saves resources by avoiding duplication of efforts.

2) Evaluation:

After information has been collected, the analyst must determine whether or not the data is useful and/or accurate. If the information emanates from an informant, the analyst should determine the informant's past reliability from the assigned investigator. Afterwards, the information may be graded and given a code which indicates source reliability. For example, a letter code could be established indicating whether the information is highly reliable, usually reliable, seldom reliable, or reliability unknown. Lastly, the evaluation portion of the intelligence cycle must be conducted in a timely fashion; otherwise, the process could become bagged down in a mass of unprocessed raw information.

3) Collation:

The third step in the process of translating information into intelligence is collation. The information has to be arranged in files so that it can be rapidly retrieved, and cross indexed so that any relationships and meanings can be recognized.

A) Collation means more than the simple storage of materials in files. It includes:

1. Sifting out of useless or non-relevant or incorrect information.

2. Orderly arrangement of collected materials so that relationships between apparently disconnected data elements may be established.

3. The creation of a system for rapid retrieval of stored or filed information.

B) Card Tile Systems should include the following:

1. Names of persons including aliases, identifying data,
(DNOP, residence, citizenship, passport data, physical description); cases involved and an indication of the role played by the subject in the case, e.g. courier, controlled, source , family connections , education, occupation, languages , indictments, arrests, court record, business affiliations, current travel and residence status, activities and whereabouts,

2. Businesses should be indexed in such a way as to provide the easiest retrieval of Information. Businesses containing the words, "Cafe", "Nightclub", "Hotel", "Restaurant" should be indexed by the name of the business rather than its type.

3. Telephone numbers should show the telephone number, followed by the city, state, or country the phone number is located in.

4. Ships and airplanes, should show, type, size, make, serial numbers, and markings.

5. Vehicles, should show license number, make, type, color, and other descriptive data available,

6. Sources of information will show only a code name and number In all reporting only the code number will appear.

The purpose for indexing in depth as described above is to provide a swift and accurate retrieval of information contained in official investigative and intelligence files. Accurate indexing is mandatory in order to obtain a clear picture of subjects, businesses, etc. (examples of all of the above will be presented during the course of instruction) .

4) Analysis

The function that assembles bits and pieces of information from many sources and puts them together to show some sort of pattern and meaning is the analysis. Without the analysis function, a piece oi : information in the files remains just that a piece of information in the files. Through research, ideas and concepts are also developed which later become the basis for hypotheses.
Hypothesis is a tentative statement of the meaning of a collection o information when arranged in a logical manner. In the process, many alternative hypotheses may be developed if the information is limited and poorly related.

5) Dissemination

The word report is used in a variety of ways by law enforcement agencies. in its most familiar form it refers to the information dispatched by patrolmen or investigators or even informers to headquarters. Such filed reports constitute inputs of information. It is essential to a comprehension of the intelligence process to understand that the information contained in field reports cannot properly be thought of as intelligence until it is evaluated, analyzed, and possibly combined with other data. Intelligence reports, as used here, refer to the end products of the intelligence process. Some may be brief, and some may be quite complex, in any case, they should be tailored to particular requirements of the users in questions.

A. The intelligence report must be objective.

b. The report should be written in such a way that there is a clear distinction between positive information or facts; those pieces which have gone into developing a hypothesis, and the conclusions which are drawn from both the facts and the hypothesis.

C. The intelligence report must have two parts:

1. An analytic statement giving the conclusions as to the meaning of the data collected in the report, answering questions, "So what"? "What does this report mean"? "Why should I read it"?

2. The second part being a summary of the information that backs up the conclusion. An abstract giving time, dates, sources, and a brief statement of the criminal activity involved.

The primary function of dissemination is to distribute the finished product or report to enforcement elements where it will be used. The most important single rule of dissemination is that intelligence analysis is delivered intact to the head of enforcement.

6) Reevaluation:

Reevaluation is the final step in the "Intelligence Process" and one which unfortunately is often forgotten or ignored. Simply, the day to day operations of the intelligence unit and the intelligence products that it disseminates to the field must be evaluated periodically.
Otherwise, there is no effective way to assess whether or not the intelligence unit has had a positive impact or provided meaningful support to field enforcement units with useful intelligence products. It is crucial that the Intelligence Chief and Enforcement
Director be able to gauge the performance of the intelligence group and measure its effectiveness, so that, any weaknesses may be promptly corrected. Enforcement depends heavily upon the intelligence function* consequently, the reevaluation step becomes quite essential by insuring the integrity of the entire process.

There must be a close cooperation between intelligence and enforcement personnel in order to create a viable working bond between the two offices.

The cycle of gathering, filing, researching, analyzing, and disseminating information is the answer to a strong intelligence oriented organization.

2 INTELLIGENCE THEORY

INTRODUCTION

Successful narcotic law enforcement is dependent upon accurate intelligence information. Federal Bureau of Investigation
Director, William Webster has said, "The only way any coordinated efforts can succeed in combatting drug trafficking, organized crime, terrorism, or even bank robberies is through the timely and candid exchange of intelligence data on criminal activities." While all of us will agree with this concept , few investigators due to the very nature of theit work, previous enforcement experiences and law enforcement training understand the basic theory of intelligence, or in other words the thinking process, intent and methodology associated with arriving at a finished intelligence product. This course will serve as an introduction to the basic theory of intelligence and will be expanded upon in following courses.

INVESTIGATION VS. INTELLIGENCE

The principal difference between investigation and intelligence is that investigation is basically evidentiary in its function.
Intelligence on the other hand is PREMONITORY; that is, its purpose is to alert, warn and provide advance information about criminal activity.

In investigative reporting, reports are evidentiary in nature and geared toward presenting statements and assembled information acquired under rules of criminal procedure, and in a format that satisfies the elements of proof needed for a successful prosecution. Investigative reports do not allow for opinions or amplifications which do not meet the evidentiary requirements.

Intelligence reports on the other hand do not necessarily have prosecution as their main objective. These reports are often intended to focus a police organization in the direction of potential criminal activity, or explain ongoing criminal activities that require specifically targeted investigations. These reports further serve to alert the police organization to future threats or trends to which a tactical coordinated response may be required.

By its nature intelligence reporting cannot be expected to meet the strict, hard fact, evidentiary standards of investigative reports, since much of the information is often dated, fragmented or obtained from sources of untested reliability. Because of these circumstances the intelligence analyst has to rely on a different standard of reasoning than the investigator. If the Intelligence officer was required to meet the same evidentiary criteria needed in investigative reports, intelligence information would tend to go unreported, since intelligence products are often based on educated opinion rather than pure evidentiary fact.

OBJECTIVES OF INTELLIGENCE (DEVELOPMENT OF INFERENCES)

The main objective of criminal intelligence is the development of valid inferences about the truth of past, present or future criminal situations. Central to the process of developing inferences is INDUCTIVE LOGIC and probability assessment which allow the analyst to go beyond the basic premises (SUPPORTIVE ARGUMENTS) to make new discoveries or predictions.

a. Types of Inferences.

(1) Hypotheses. A tentative explanation; A theory that requires additional information for confirmation or denial.

(2) Conclusion is an explanation that is well supported; a hypothesis that has been confirmed and which can be acted upon.

(3) Prediction is an inference about something that will happen in the future.

(4) Estimation. An inference made from a sample to the whole.

DEDUCTIVE VS. INDUCTIVE LOGIC

a. In investigation the officer relies on deductive logic in arriving at the answer. Utilizing deductive logic the inferences developed through investigation do not go beyond the premises; if the premises are true, the Inference must be true. Deductive logic, in common usage, is to go from the general to the specific.

Ex. 1. Deductive Logic

Premise: Heroin is an addictive drug.

Premise: Peter Kim uses heroin on a daily basis.

Inference: Peter Kim is a heroin addict.

Ex. 2.
Premise: The shades are drawn.

Premise: The doors are locked.

Premise: No one answers the door,

Premise: The garage is empty.

Inference: No one is home.

b. In arriving at a finished intelligence product the analyst relies on INDUCTIVE logic. In INDUCTIVE logic the inference goes beyond the premises; if the premises are true, the inference is probably true (but also it is possibly false). Inductive logic, in common usage, is to go from the specific to the general.

Ex. INDUCTIVE LOGIC
Premise: Hong Kong, Europe and the United States are the primary markets for illicit SE Asian Heroin.

Premise: Burma, Laos and Thailand are the primary producers of opium in SE Asia.

Premise: Opium is converted into heroin in Burma, Laos and Thailand.

Premise: The 1986 opium crop in Burma, Laos and Thailand is expected to greatly exceed the opium crop produced during the 1984 and 1985 seasons.

Inference: Heroin production in Burma, Laos and Thailand will increase during 1986 with a corresponding increase in attempts to smuggle heroin into Hong Kong, Europe and the United States.

USE OF SYLLOGISMS

a. As illustrated in the preceding examples of deductive and inductive logic, the use of a syllogism is a useful tool for analyzing arguments (Premises) and for developing inferences. In a formal SYLLOGISM, the premises, obtained by summarizing all relevant information, are stated as clearly as possible and listed one below the other. A line is drawn below the final premise with the inference(s) stated below this line. Just like the total in an addition problem the inference (s) stated below the line is what the premises above the line add up to.

Ex. SYLLOGISM

Premise:

Premise:

Premise:

Premise:

Premise:

Inference:

EVALUATION OF PREMISES (Argument)

a. The quality of the finished intelligence product depends directly on the premises that support the inference(s) . Premise VALIDITY then, is mainly a function of data evaluation. The more certain the premises, the more accurate is the inference(s) developed.

b. Practical approach to developing inferences:

(1) Use all applicable, relevant information.

(2) Describe and integrate fragmented information.

(3) Formulate premises,

(4) Develop alternative hypothesis.

(5) Use probability values to assess certainty.

(6) Avoid logical fallacies.

PROBABILITY ASSESSMENT

a. In general, probability is a decimal fraction that indicates the likelihood that an event will happen (or that a condition exists) , Here* probability is the likelihood that an inference is valid (true). An inference without an assessment of the premise validity is incomplete.

Probability (P) = Number of times the event will occur /Number of opportunities for the event to occur.

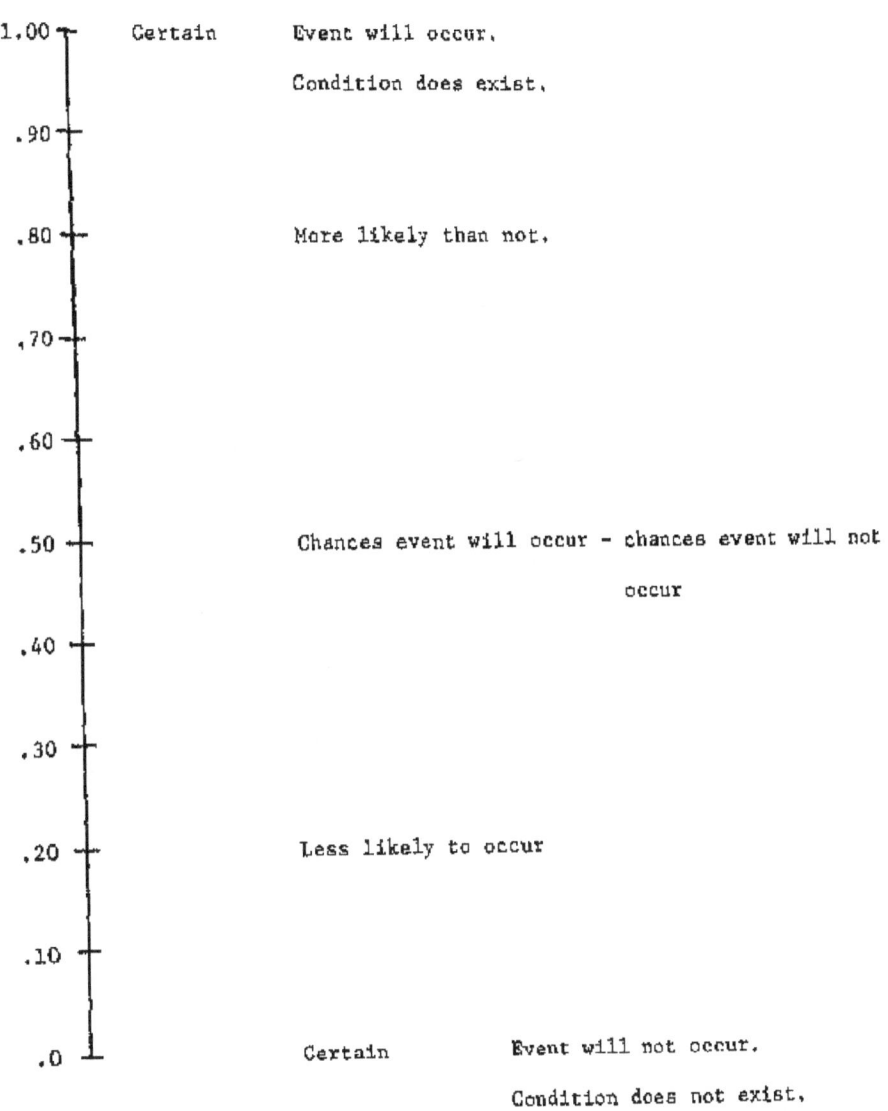

1.00 — Certain   Event will occur.

Condition does exist.

.90 —

.80 —   More likely than not.

.70 —

.60 —

.50 —   Chances event will occur - chances event will not

occur

.40 —

.30 —

.20 —   Less likely to occur

.10 —

.0 —   Certain   Event will not occur.

Condition does not exist.

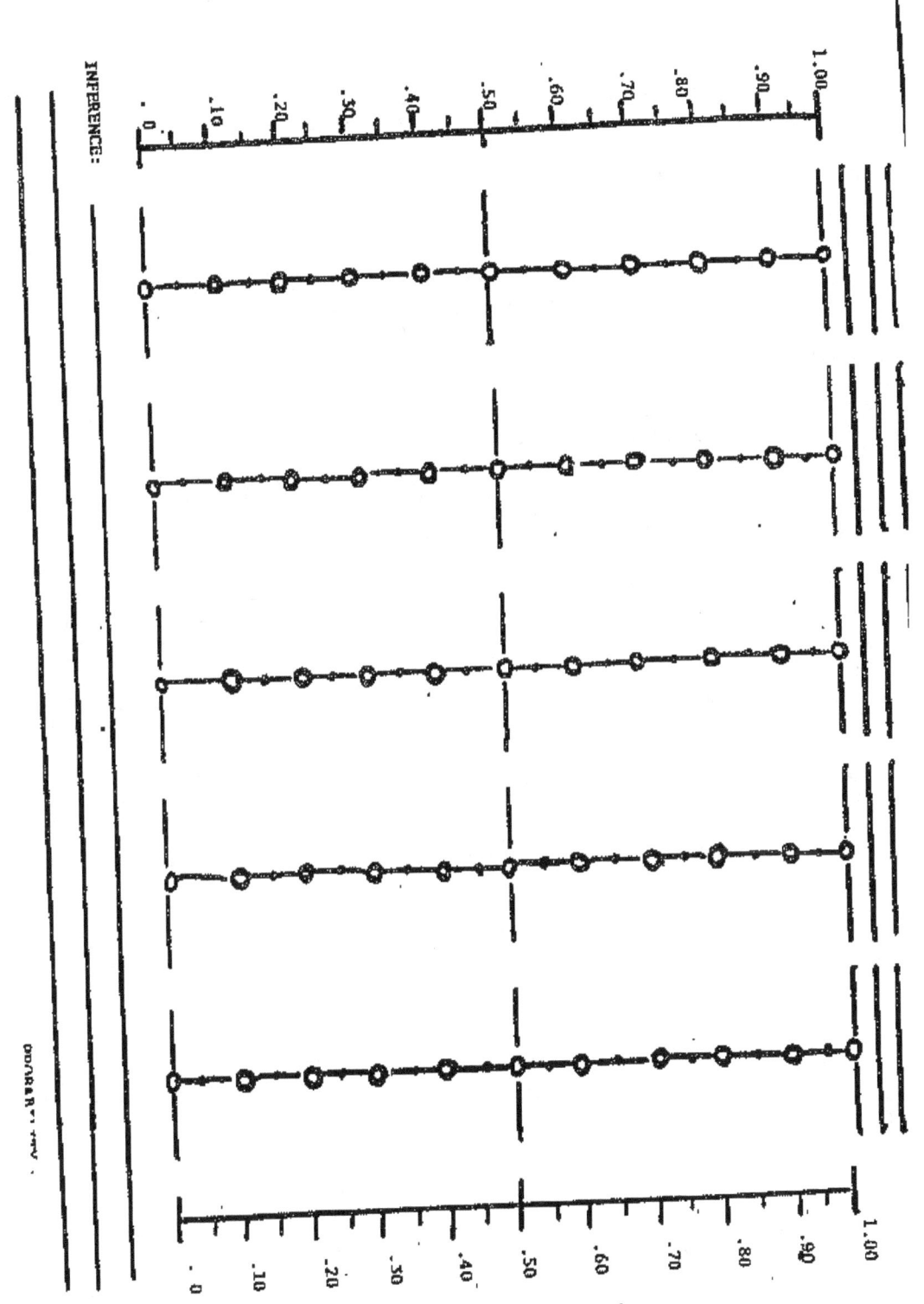

FALLACIES RESULTING FROM INCORRECT LOGIC

There are several types of errors that an analyst might commit during the reasoning process. The errors result in false inferences and are called fallacies. The most common fallacies fall into one of two general classes - omissions and false assumptions.

a. Fallacies of Omission.

Fallacies in this category are those that omit some important premise, consideration, or aspect of an argument. Within this category are the fallacies of oversimplification, inadequate sampling, mistaken cause, and false dilemma.

(1) Oversimplification: An inference that fails to account adequately for the entire complex conditions under consideration.

(2) Inadequate sampling: A fallacy produced by drawing inferences (estimates) from samples that are too few or from samples that are not truly representative.

(3) Mistaken cause: An unwarranted cause and effect relationship established between events or conditions that coincidentally exist at the same time or precede one another.

(4) False dilemma: A fallacy in which only the extreme alternatives are considered.

b. Fallacies of False Assumptions*

Examples of fallacies involving errors in assumptions are 1 , begging the question, establishing hypotheses contrary to fact, and the misuse of analogies.

(1) Begging the question: Instead of responding to the question or problem, the question is rephrased or the problem is replaced with another.

(2) Hypothesis contrary to fact: A fallacy that occurs when someone states decisively what would have happened had the circumstance been different, providing a hypothesis that cannot he verified.

(3) Misused analogies: When reasoning from analogy, the analyst assumes that the object or event in the real world is similar to the object or event in the analogy. Analogies are inappropriate as evidence or proof in analytical work. Analogies are most appropriately used for helping to explain or clarify a concept.

SUMMARY

The theory of criminal intelligence can be compared to the assembly of a picture with the individual premises developed from collected information representing the individual pieces of the puzzle. The more pieces we assemble the clearer the total picture becomes.

In the intelligence process, however, seldom will all the necessary information be available to complete the entire picture, at least in the initial intelligence product. However, once the associations and workings of a criminal organization or activity start to surface the intelligence information gaps will become evident to the analyst. Many of these gaps can be filled by tasking investigators to develop specific information in the specific areas required, thus serving to further fortify the intelligence information.

As in the case of our picture puzzle it is not necessary to have all the pieces of the puzzle in order to identify the total picture. If enough relevant information, summarized into sound premises is developed and analyzed, valid meanings of associations and workings of the targeted Criminal organization will emerge thereby allowing for a tactical response to the activity discovered.

3 INTELLIGENCE COLLECTION

INTRODUCTION

A survey of current public opinion leads unequivocally to the opinion that the war against the narcotics traffic has been lost by law enforcement. Every day one can find news articles on previously unheard of quantities of all types of drugs being found or seized. These seizures represent only the tip of the iceberg in terms of the actual volume of illegal drugs which are being produced and sold, but which evade the attention of police authorities. It can be safely concluded that the drug menace is a more significant threat to civilized societies than ever before. This situation exists in spite of increased efforts on the part of law enforcement authorities worldwide to stem the tide.

Part of the explanation for this crisis in the drug situation is the lack of sophisticated, long range, in depth, intelligence collection techniques applied to narcotics law enforcement in the same manner that these techniques are applied to other areas of human endeavor. There has been a relative failure to concentrate efforts and resources on the identification, recruitment, and training of potential human sources of intelligence far enough in advance to provide a proactive approach to narcotics law enforcement.

The investigation of narcotics trafficking presents a unique challenge to the investigator. As opposed to investigating a specific crime with a specific solution, e.g., robbery, murder, etc., the narcotics officer Investigates crimes which are fluid and ongoing in nature. For that reason a proactive approach is necessary to obtain significant results or one is forever "chasing one's tail." The continual reliance on traditional methods of narcotics enforcement, e.g., buy-bust, surveillance, etc., has not been productive in terms of major program objectives. The primary goal of narcotics enforcement programs is the immobilization of large trafficking organizations with significant impact on the supply of illicit drugs available to the consumer.

All law enforcement agencies are aware of the insignificant effect on the traffic of the arrest of couriers and other lower echelon elements of the various trafficking groups. In addition, the occasional successful immobilization of one or two top figures only creates space at the top of the organization for aspiring group members. To be truly effective the immobilization effort must be directed against the entire organization. The "Pizza Connection" case in the United States led to large-scale arrests of organized crims members in Sicily which now threaten the very structure of the Mafia in their own ancient stronghold. In order to accomplish significant law enforcement goals and objectives similar to those in that case, it becomes necessary to employ long range, sophisticated techniques geared toward the production of intelligence which can support those types of law enforcement operations.

The objective of this course is to familiarize the student with the twelve basic principles of intelligence collection and indicate how these principles can be applied in the specific area of drug enforcement.
Also, recognizing that human intelligence sources are the key to this effort, considerable attention is devoted to the development and management of these sources in terms of maximizing results given limited resources. These objectives lead toward the evolution of a greater utilization of sophisticated intelligence collection activities with greater ultimate impact on the narcotics traffic.

Twelve Basic Principles of Intelligence Collection

1. Sponsor

All intelligence collection activities must begin with a sponsor.
The sponsor is the ultimate client for the finished intelligence product.
Simply defined the sponsor is the agency or government which is behind the
collection effort. For example, the United States Government, through
Congress, orders the Department of Justice to do something about the drug
problem. Justice then sets guidelines for proceeding to deal with the problem
and tasks DEA. DEA then carries out Department of Justice policies and
objectives in this area. The actual sponsor can be said to be the U.S.
Government.

The sponsor, as the ultimate client, establishes the intelligence
requirements and then provides the resources necessary to conduct the
collection effort. The intelligence requirements for DEA are to provide the
necessary information for the successful immobilization of major trafficking
groups. By the same token major traffickers act as sponsors when they task
elements of their organizations to infiltrate law enforcement agencies and
provide intelligence on what strategies law enforcement authorities are using
against them. As will be seen throughout this course, the traffickers are
also in the intelligence business and frequently use these same techniques
against US. It is valuable to always keep that in mind.

When prioritizing objectives in the utilization of resources on a daily basis
, it becomes relatively simple to lose sight of primary goals.
Intelligence collection efforts must always take into account the sponsor and
the sponsor's requirements in terms of results. The sponsor, whoever it may
be depending upon government or country, is usually paying the bill, and
therefore it is the sponsor's requirements which are paramount if the
continuity of the program is to be insured.

2. Targets/Objectives

The target of an intelligence gathering operation is self-explanatory. In our
case the targets are the major drug trafficking organizations. It is
important to keep in mind that the sophisticated, intelligence collection
techniques discussed in this course are, by their very nature, conplex and
time consuming. They are not intended to be used against the lower level drug
dealers in that the time and resources invested are not justified by results
obtained. In terms of the higher level, large-scale trafficking groups,
however, which are not so easily compromised through traditional techniques,
a long term intelligence operation may be the only effective measure
available to law enforcement. In this case the end certainly justifies the
means.

The objectives of the mission against the target are clearly to disrupt their activities and eventually neutralize the organization.

While we may represent different sponsors and though our individual targets may differ, as law enforcement personnel, our objectives are the same. It is wise to remember that in a proactive approach to drug enforcement, we start with an identified target and proceed from there,

To function by relying upon a source of information to identify the potential targets usually leads to a fragmented, reactive approach concentrated on a lower level of the traffic. It is best to analyze all available intelligence to determine the major trafficking groups and to then target those groups for subsequent investigation. In other words, start with the target and proceed to look for sources of information. Do not start with a source of information and proceed to look for targets.

3. Sources

a. Purpose of Human Sources

Inevitably when discussing the subject of human sources with other narcotics investigators, the content iff made that the risks and problems involved in the use of these sources outweigh their usefulness. This outlook ignores the simple fact that sources who have been properly assessed and recruited represent the most effective weapon available to law enforcement against the drug traffic* The reasons for this are obvious. Sources can provide intelligence to investigators from are not available to the investigator. For example, the freight manager at an airline can report on the movement of goods and personnel; a salesclerk at a pharmaceutical supply house can report on suspicious purchases of laboratory equipment or precursor materials. In some cases the source is actively involved with traffickers. A source in a clandestine laboratory can report on production and distribution schedules; a pilot flying for the organization can report on pickup and delivery schedules, clandestine airstrips, members of the organization, etc. It is often difficult to penetrate an organization from the outside without compromising the investigation.

Human sources can often report from within ethnic areas that are difficult to penetrate; e.g., Chinese trafficking organizations, militant or terrorist groups. The human source, while pretending to be part of the trafficking group is actually reporting firsthand "knowledge of who, what, when, where, and how to the investigator. This information would be extremely difficult to obtain by other means. The source can also eventually assist the investigator in penetrating the organization himself, in an undercover capacity, by introducing the investigator as a trusted accomplice and vouching for him. This provides the investigator with direct access to the target.

b. Types of Sources

There are fundamentally three types of human sources. The first type is the "support" source. This represents any individual who provides information which assists the intelligence operation. These people generally operate in an overt fashion. They are able to provide valuable information by virtue of their particular situation or employment; e.g., a hotel desk clerk, an airline reservationist or ticket agent, or a bartender. These 1 sources are the easiest to manage in that they require very little supervision.

The second type of source is the "Action" source or what is commonly thought of as an informant. The source is acting directly under the supervision of the investigator and is usually operating in a covert or undercover capacity. Thin is the type of source who usually is a member of or has infiltrated the target group and can provide firsthand knowledge of the group's activities. This type of source requires the greatest degree of supervision in that his mission is extremely delicate from the standpoint of personal danger and also due to the possibility of compromise of the entire investigation. Examples of this type of source are a courier employed by the traffickers, a chemist working in a clandestine laboratory, or a pilot hired to transport the contraband drugs.

The last type of intelligence source is the "Principal" source. This type of source is extremely important in terms of the development of intelligence networks. The principal source's main role is to recruit other action and support sources thereby constructing a network of intelligence sources who all report to the principal source. The principal source then communicates the collected intelligence to the investigator. The action and support sources are not aware of each other's roles as sources and do not know the investigator. This concept will be discussed further in the section on compartmentation. A good example of a principal source is the supervisor of baggage and cargo handlers at an international airport. The investigator is aware of trafficking activity conducted by smuggling drugs in the cargo and baggage of international flights. The investigator then recruits the cargo supervisor as a principal source. The supervisor recruits baggage and cargo handlers on each shift to report suspicious activities. In this way, the investigator has intelligence sources working around the clock to provide information without arousing the suspicion that surveillance might incur,

c. Source Motivation

In the development and management of human sources, the investigator must consider those factors which motivated the subject to assist in the investigation in the first place. These factors are important for they provide the investigator with the incentives he needs to properly manage the source. In addition, these factors alert the astute investigator to possible dangers involved in the utilization of any particular source.

The most common motivator is material. The source provides information in exchange for some form of reward; e.g., money, vehicle, official favors, etc. The hazard in utilizing this type of source, who works for purely mercenary reasons, is the possibility that the traffickers will provide a greater financial incentive, and the source may compromise the investigation or provide the investigator with false or misleading information. The same situation could occur if the source receives less reward from the investigator than he feels he is entitled to and becomes embittered. The investigator must always be cognizant to these risks when dealing with this type of individual.

A second common motivator is emotion. The source cooperates and assists the investigator from fear, hate, revenge, love, prestige or some other similar emotional factor. For example, the paramour of one of the principal figures in the trafficking organization feels mistreated, neglected or rejected. She provides information to get revenge. Perhaps a relative of a member of the trafficking group wants revenge from some misfortune which befell the family due to the individual's participation in the group. Some individuals thrive upon the prestige they feel they acquire by associating with law enforcement authorities. These people will often become sources to develop that association, although the likelihood that this type of individual can have the type of access to a trafficking group necessary for an action source is questionable. Prestige motivated sources generally are more likely to be support sources .

One particular danger in this area is the individual who contacts the investigator and expresses a desire to assist by providing intelligence on the operations of an identified trafficking group. This individual claims that he is against drugs and has some particular hatred for the group in question. He states that he wants no financial compensation for his services but only wants to help the police eliminate this trafficking group. The investigator must be alert to the possibility that this individual may be a member of a rival trafficking group. The information provided is intended to eliminate competition rather than actually do anything about the volume of drugs available.

d. Establishment

Upon initial contact with any source of information, the establishment procedure, by which the subject becomes an active part of the investigative process, represents the most important phase of the entire proceeding. Adequate time spent during this stage can prevent serious errors which could jeopardize the entire investigation at some future date.

The first step of the source establishment procedure is to thoroughly identify the individual. This can be done through fingerprints and photographs. Code names and aliases can be provided to protect the source's true identity. For most sources the fact that their true names and identities will not be revealed is a primary concern. Through the use of photographs r fingerprints and code names, sources can conclusively be identified at any time in the future, and their past record of utilization can be verified. Also, other offices and branches of your organization can verify a source 's claims of previous or current utilization in intelligence collection operations through the identity procedure accomplished at the subject's initial establishment.

The next step of the procedure is the completion of a personal history statement. A typical personal history form is included in Example 1 of this section. The information in this form is valuable in providing a concise look at the subject's background. It also provides valuable information which could assist in locating the subject in the future should that become necessary. A separate criminal record check with all appropriate police agencies should be done to determine if the source has been involved in criminal activity, or if the source is currently wanted by any agency for outstanding crimes. This information is essential to avoid possible embarrassment or, more seriously, the development of an incident which could endanger someone's life.

The last stage of the establishment procedure is the completion of a thorough debriefing report which will contain all the intelligence the source is prepared to offer. This report can also reflect the source's potential for future activity and identify probable targets toward which the source will be directed. This information can also be included in a succinct statement in the personal history form if that proves more desirable from the standpoint of the reporting requirements of the individual agency. In that case, the establishment report would' contain only the intelligence information provided by the potential source. The investigator should proceed carefully and thoroughly during the interview to avoid inadvertently missing or omitting details which could be vital at some later stage of the investigation. A source debriefing guide is included in Example 2 and can greatly assist during this initial interview.

e. Management of Sources

Subsequent to initial contact with the source by the agency and the establishment procedure, the supervision of the utilization of the source becomes an important factor. This responsibility generally falls upon the first line supervisor of the investigator handling the source.
This supervisory oversight is critical in order to 'avoid the kinds of problems which occasionally occur where either the investigator is unaware of the source's efforts to manipulate him or becomes personally involved with the source to the degree that the investigator's judgment in the handling of the source becomes suspect. The supervisor must be aware that the investigator and the source will work closely together, often times under considerable stress. It is inevitable that a strong personal relationship will develop. The management of the source through the first line supervisor can provide the checks and balances which are necessary to maintain a proper and objective perspective.

The first of these checks and balances is the mandatory supervisory approval of any potential source of information prior to that source's utilization. The investigator conducts the establishment procedure but does not give the source any instructions other than to await further contact. The supervisor then reviews the criminal record checks, personal history form, establishment report and any other relevant information. Once the. supervisor is satisfied that the utilization of the source is warranted and meets the agency guidelines, the investigator is instructed to proceed.

The supervisor's responsibilities do not end with approval for utilization. The supervisor must continue to monitor the source's activities throughout his utilization. One method of insuring this active monitoring is to require the supervisor to be present during a thorough debriefing of every active source of information at least once every ninety days. This introduces an objective, dispassionate listener to the debriefing process at designated intervals and helps to reduce the possibility of problems developing due to the relationship between the investigator and the source.

The supervisor should also personally review all active source files at least once every ninety days. The source file will contain all documents, reports, memoranda, etc., pertaining to the source. One very important type of document is the receipt of payment to the source for information provided or services rendered. Payments have always been a potential trouble area. The agency must have some method for showing payment to an informant and that the payment was properly received. This is necessary for internal agency review in case a particular source claims that he did not receive remuneration. The supervisor and the investigator both sign the appropriate form which the source also signs upon receipt of the payment. That payment is witnessed by all three subjects. An example of a type of payment form which can be used for this purpose is included in Example 3.

When reviewing a source's active file, the supervisor can compare records of payment to intelligence received or services provided. In this way the supervisor can easily determine if the results of the source T s efforts justify the cost of his utilization. The supervisor can also determine, by the amount and frequency of payment, as compared to source productivity, whether or not some irregularity might exist in the way the investigator is handling the subject. This is especially important where first line supervisors are transferred frequently which disrupts the continuity of the reviewing process.

4. Recruitment

Now that the concept of the human source has been elaborated it becomes necessary to consider the various methods of source recruitment.
All intelligence collection activity is improved through growth. That growth requires a constant, dedicated effort toward identification and subsequent recruitment of productive sources of information. As stated earlier, the establishment of the target or objective precedes the recruitment. This will insure that recruited sources will have access to or can act against determined targets.

The first stage of the recruitment cycle is that of "spotting" or recognizing a potential source of information. This is a constant, ongoing process where the investigator is always looking for sources who can provide information about the target. The recognition can come about as a result of a tip from other sources, surveillance of the target and his/her activities, or perhaps from the source itself who volunteers his/her assistance. The information the source may be able to provide can be immediate or it may have future application. The investigator should always keep long range goals in mind. One basic principle to remember is that it is usually better to recruit someone who is already in place vis-a-vis the target rather than someone who will have to infiltrate from outside. This spotting activity is often time consuming and requires considerable patience, but the investigator must remember that these types of investigations are not spur of the moment. If significant results are to be realized, then a cautious, painstaking approach must be employed.

The second phase of the recruitment cycle is the assessment of the potential source in terms of possible motivation, capabilities, access to objectives, and liabilities. Each factor must be carefully weighed prior to any attempt to recruitment. For example, surveillance of a major trafficker reveals that he has frequent arguments with his wife over his late night activities, etc. We could conclude that perhaps she is angry enough or jealous enough to motivate her to provide information on her husband which is of interest to us. We must remember, however, that anger is quickly dissipated and jealousy assuaged through simple acts of consideration. A recruitment attempt, ill-timed, could result in the compromise of the ongoing investigation. The assessment process should be thoroughly analyzed by the investigator to avoid rash actions.

Once the assessment is completed satisfactorily, an in depth investigation of the potential source should be done. The possible motivation of the potential source should be determined and then corroborated if possible. Also, the investigator needs to know if the potential source is actually working for someone else; e.g. , another investigator or agency. This will avoid duplication of effort or conflict of interest. More important, the investigator needs to consider and investigate the possibility that the potential source is actually working for the opposition. In this case, the source's real motivation will be the penetration of the police agency in order to further the aims of the trafficker. The investigator must always be cognizant of the fact that the twelve basic principles of intelligence collection are often applied against the sponsor and agency by the traffickers, with greater resources in some cases.

The final stage of the recruitment cycle is the actual recruitment approach itself. There are several different strategies, and the best one to use is always dictated by the unique set of circumstances presented in each individual case.

The first technique is the "close" or "developmental" approach. This is an unhurried technique which presupposes a long term effort. The investigator invests the time necessary to develop a personal relationship with the potential source. That friendship is then used as the basis for the recruitment approach. This type of strategy is appropriate in those cases where the investigator will be dealing closely and regularly with thp source. It is especially appropriate for the recruitment of principal sources. The danger in this technique is that the investigator will allow himself to get too close to the source and reveal operational details which the source has no need to know. The supervisor must carefully monitor the handling of these types of sources. While they are usually the most reliable sources, the security of the investigation must always be preserved.

The second type of strategy, and perhaps the most contnon in law enforcement, is the "cold pitch 1 ' or "distant" approach. Here the constraints of time or the press of events do not allow the development of a long term relationship. The potential source is directly approached and his or her assistance is solicited. In this type of approach the assessment and investigation phases of the recruitment cycle are vital. It is here where the possibility of error, which could compromise the investigation, is greatest. Once satisfied, however, the recruitment effort can go forward. Ther^ is always going to be a certain degree of risk, but that risk can be minimized by a thorough assessment and investigation.

The third strategy is the combination technique. Here, the investigator does the spotting, assessment and investigation of the potential source. When the timing is right the investigator has someone else make the recruitment approach. That someone else is usually a principal source. In this fashion, if the recruitment fails, neither the agency nor the investigator is compromised. A potential drawback is that the investigator will not have a direct access to the source. In that sense this technique may be appropriate for support or action sources where the investigator directs their activities through the principal source. The security of the overall operation is thereby enhanced.

The final strategy is the "False Flag" approach. This technique works well in those situations where the spotting process reveals that the source would be highly productive and is motivated against the target but would never consent to cooperate with the authorities. This refusal may be due to an antiestablishment attitude or a particular repugnance for a specific agency on the basis of some previous experience. Regardless, a recruitment effort under these circumstances is bound to fail unless the real sponsor can be disguised. For example, in many cases the potential source is approached by a principal source and is led to believe that he is assisting a rival trafficking organization. In some cases, potential sources who distinctly anti police, but very patriotic are are told that they are assisting a military intelligence against traffickers who are also involved with terrorists. Although somewhat more complex, this type of strategy can be very productive in terms of potential sources who would otherwise be inaccessible. Great care must be taken to prevent the source from discovering the real sponsor or the revenge factor could be extremely harmful to the sponsor.

5. Compartmentation

This basic principle concerns the separation of all the various sources of information. This is done in order to prevent each source fron knowing anything about any of the other sources in the intelligence network. Only the investigator will know the identities of all the sources. The principal sources will also know the sub sources being managed under their control. The idea is that principal sources should not be aware of the existence of other principal sources nor of the networks controlled by the other principal sources. By the same token the support and action sources will not be aware of each other nor will they be cognizant of the investigator. The action and support sources, also known as subsources, will only know their respective principal source. The following diagram is an example of a typical intelligence network:

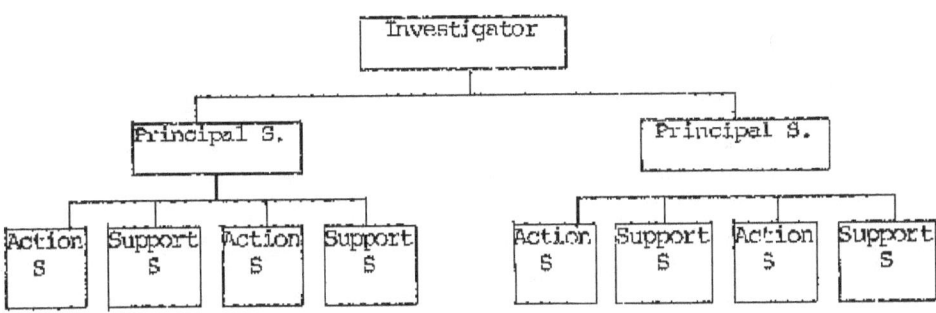

The Compartmentation principle is a vital one for the following reasons. First of all it facilitates the verification or corroboration of information being provided. Many times the investigator is forced to accept the source's information at face value, because the investigator does not have the same access as the source. If there are several independent sources with similar access to the same information, but who are unaware of each other, then one source can be tasked regarding information already provided by a different source. If both reports coincide, then the original intelligence has been corroborated. This is extremely useful for periodically checking source veracity.

Another important reason for compartmentation is the security of the entire intelligence collection network. It should be obvious that through the principle of compartmentation, if an active source is recruited by the traffickers, that source's ability to compromise the investigation is considerably limited. By the same token, surveillance of sources by traffickers or other opposition agencies can cause only limited damage. The overall idea is to integrate security into the structure of the intelligence network, and compartmentation accomplishes this. The risk of entire networks being revealed is considerably lessened.

6. Handling

Handling refers to the actual direction and control of the source by the investigator. The first concern of the investigation, subsequent to recruitment, should be training. The investigator has the responsibility to train his sources in the techniques necessary for completion of any operation. It is not reasonable to assume that just because a source has access to certain information r he will automatically realize what is and what is not of importance to the investigator. For example, a source at the fuel ramp of an airport might provide a detailed, daily report on the number and type of private aircraft landing and taking off, as well as number of passengers and time of day. The same source might also, however, neglect to note the aircraft registration number.

The investigator must be prepared to give sources specific assignments with clearly understood objectives. The source must be trained to recognize what types of information are most beneficial to the investigator in terms of the particular operation. It is vital that the investigator not assume that the source automatically realizes this. If not properly trained, valuable opportunities for the collection of significant intelligence may be missed. The source debriefing guide, contained in the appendix, can assist the investigator in alerting the source as to what type of information is most important.

Another aspect of source handling is the periodic debriefing conducted by the investigator. This debriefing should be done for all active sources with certain regularity; e.g., every thirty days, whether or not the source believes he has anything new to report. Many times the source has learned something which he believes is inconsequential, but when added to other information received from other sources, that same information proves to be highly enlightening. In addition, the periodic debriefing provides the investigator with the opportunity to reaffirm his relationship with the source and to keep current on the source's status. This enhances the agency's control over the various sources contributing to the overall operation. As previously mentioned, the investigator's supervisor should personally attend at least one of these regular debrief ings every ninety days.

Whenever or wherever these debrief ings take place, any significant contacts with sources, should always be thoroughly documented. The investigator should not rely strictly on his memory. It may someday become an issue as to whether or not the contact ever took place. This is especially important for payments. Ml payments should be witnessed to avoid the possibility of allegations that the source never received the payment or did not receive the full amount. Debriefing reports, which receive wide circulation, can utilize the source's code name, provided at establishment, to avoid revealing the source's true identity. Payment receipts should be signed by the informant in his true name as these records can be kept in the informant's file in a safe place. There is no need for circulation of this information, but it is always available for internal review by qualified agency personnel.

When handling human sources, the investigator should be aware of common recurring problems regarding utilization; e.g., false or misleading information. The source may actually be working for the trafficker and has penetrated the intelligence collection operation for the express purpose of leading the investigation astray. This type of strategy is called a provocation and will be discussed in detail later.
If the source is receiving remuneration for his information, he may tell the investigator whatever he believes the investigator will pay the most for, whether or not it is accurate or true. The source might also have a revenge motive and wants to hamper the agency's operations.

Whatever the motive r the investigator needs to develop ways of corroborating or verifying the information provided by sources. This can be done through other, independent sources of information, through surveillance, through requiring the source to provide tangible evidence supporting the intelligence; e.g., photographs, recordings, etc. and occasionally through polygraph examination where possible. These precautions will enable the investigator to maintain an acceptable level of confidence in his information.

Another potential problem area is the theft of agency funds or information. Large sums of show or flash money are often utilized in narcotics investigations. Some individuals pretend to assist the agency in the development of an investigation in the hopes of creating a situation where they will have access to these funds and be able to abscond. Others hope to acquire classified information regarding agency operations and targets in order to sell this information to the criminal underworld. The investigator should always take the necessary precautions to prevent sources from having access to agency resources which they don't actually require to complete their own particular mission.

The investigator must be aware of the possibility of the involvement of the source in illegal activity. The source my be trafficking himself and hopes to hide that fact by his association with the agency. The source may feel that if he is apprehended in the commission of some crime, his relationship with the investigator or the agency will provide him with immunity. All human sources must be made to clearly understand that at no tinR are they to engage in any activity r which could be construed to be illegal, unless under the specific direction of the investigator; e.g., undercover negotiations, etc. It is best to have every source sign a declaration to this effect, perhaps on the personal history form at the tune of establishment.

Other problems which can arise from the handling of sources are the compromise of the investigator's or other agency personnel's identities to the opposition. This allows the traffickers to begin to mount surveillance operations of their own. Also, due to some hidden motive, the source may be pretending to assist the investigator merely to set him or her up for reprisal action by the traffickers. For that reason, the investigator must always temper trust of any source with a certain degree of caution. The investigator should avoid placing himself in circumstances where the source has complete control of the situation. Some sources, possibly drug users themselves, will create problems by attempting to solicit money or drugs from the target, utilizing the situation to the source's advantage. This severely damages the source's future credibility and could lead to a dangerous confrontation, with the investigator caught in the middle.

The final potential problem area is that of females and juvenile sources. The relationships which develop between females and investigators, as well as the possibility of allegations of misconduct, require special precautions in this area. The investigator must make certain not to be placed in a compromising situation when dealing with female sources. If a male investigator is utilizing a female source, it is wise to always have another investigator witness all contacts and have these contacts thoroughly documented. The investigator should also be aware that previous experience has demonstrated that the allegiance of female sources is particularly fragile. While she may be working for the agency today, she could very well be working just as hard for the opposition tomorrow.

Juvenile sources should be seldom utilized due to the possible problems which can arise by encouraging their association with the criminal element. In addition, their judgment is invariably more suspect. In some cases the unique contribution which a juvenile source can make to an operation outweighs these considerations, but those cases are very rare.

The final aspect in the handling of human sources that the investigator and the supervisor need to consider is the possible risk to the operation produced by terminating the source's relationship to the agency. At some point in every investigation a source's continued affiliation with the agency is no longer warranted. The source's original and current motivation for assisting the investigation must be carefully reexamined. On the basis of that reexamination, a plan for the termination of the source's utilization should be carefully evolved. This is to prevent the development of attitudes on the part of thp source which are antithetical to agency objectives and interests. A disgruntled former source, who is privy to many of the agency's operating procedures, can seriously damage or hinder investigations in progress.

7 Communications

a. Systems of Communication

In the conduct of intelligence collection, the investigator must concern himself with the development of systems of communication in order to insure an orderly flow of information between the agency and respective sources. These systems will take into consideration the necessary security required to prevent exposure of the source, thereby compromising his mission, but will also allow adequate opportunity for frequent contact between the source and the investigator.

The first system is known simply as the "usual 11 or "regular" system. This is the normal, established method of communicating with the source. A location should be pre designated. While it is tempting, from the standpoint of convenience, to merely have the source report periodically to the investigator's office, this practice should be avoided. Remember, the traffickers are engaged in their own intelligence collection efforts against us. Those efforts can include surveillance of the investigator's office or possibly an informer working in some capacity in the agency office who can report on the movements of individuals into and out of the area. The risk of compromise is significantly minimized if meetings are held elsewhere.

The investigator should find a secure location for each source, remembering the principle of compartmentation. These locations need not be highly sophisticated nor necessarily costly; e.g., safe houses r etc.
Often, a safe place where both the investigator and source can drive or walk while checking for surveillance en route will suffice. Face to face meetings are always preferable. These personal contacts reduce the possibility of misunderstanding and help to strengthen and reaffirm the bond between the

investigator and the informant. Also, changes in behavior or attitude on the part of the source, observed by the investigator during these meetings, can alert the investigator to the possibility of deception or some other problem concerning the source. These clues or signs would be lost if the communication were strictly telephonic or written. Once the location is agreed upon, a regular schedule should be established. For example, the meeting could take place every Tuesday at two o'clock in the afternoon at the location. Both parties know when and where, and the communication is facilitated.

The second system of communication is the "alternate" or "secondary" system. This will accommodate changes in the patterns of the "usual" meetings when such changes become necessary. It may be that for sane reason the location, day, or tine is not convenient for a particular meeting. An alternate meeting site, day or tine will have already been agreed upon. A simple telephone call or other message, suitably coded, can alert either party to the change. It is not necessary to go into the details of the change since that has already been worked out.

The third system of communication is the "emergency" system.
Occasions may arise where either the investigator or the source needs to make contact urgently and cannot wait for the normally scheduled meeting.
It may be that the source has a particularly perishable intelligence item or the investigator may need to alert the source to some important event which is about to occur. There may also be the need to communicate some type of warning. To accommodate these circumstances, the investigator and the source should establish some type of signal. Upon receipt of this signal each party will proceed, within a certain time frame, to a pre-designated location where the meeting will take place. This emergency provision is a vital element of the communication system and should always be included in the initial arrangements made between the investigator and source.

The last system is the "reserve" system. This is a method by which individuals, who are not known to each other, can make contact without the risk of compromise. An example, of this type of situation is where a source is conducting an intelligence gathering mission in a geographic area away from the primary investigator. The source may need to contact other agency representatives in that area to pass on important information. Both, the source and the other office personnel need to be provided with signals and recognition signs; for example, standing in front of certain restaurant at a certain time holding a certain magazine.
The mutually recognizable signals enable both source and other office personnel to conclusively identify each other,

b. Means of Communications

Once times, dates, and locations have been arranged, the actual means of communication must be decided. As previously stated, the personal meeting is the preferred means of communication. The investigator should decide upon the location, time, alternate sites, cover measures and necessary security. This is to prevent the source having too much control over the situation. Any serious objections to any of these details by the source should be considered, but the investigator should make the final decisions.

Another means of communication is the "dead drop." This is utilized when the risks involved make a personal meeting or other direct contact inadvisable. An example of this is where the source has infiltrated a particularly sensitive area of the trafficker's operation.

For his own security, the trafficker may maintain a close scrutiny over the source's activities. The source still needs some way of communicating his intelligence to the investigator. Direct contact is ruled out. The dead drop can solve this problem. Both the source and investigator agree, in advance, upon a location where the source can leave messages to be retrieved at a later time by the investigator.

Also, some signal must be arranged, which the investigator can observe, indicating to nun that the drop contains information; e.g., shade on source's bedroom window pulled halfway down. By the same token the investigator needs to signal the source that the information was retrieved; e.g., crayon mark on a specified park bench. In this way information can be passed with little risk of detection.

The dead drop should be chosen with certain considerations in mind. It should be a site with natural cover making surveillance of the exact spot difficult. The source should have precise instructions as to its location. The effects of weather or other environmental circumstances upon the site should be considered. The area should be one where both the source and the investigator have access, and it is logical or not unreasonable for either of them to be there. A very good site for a dead drop is in a public rest room in a bar or restaurant.

A variation of the dead drop is the "human drop" where an intermediary receives the message from the source and later passes it on to the investigator. This is an effective method of communicating without the risk of unauthorized individuals accidentally finding the information as could happen in the dead drop situation. The drawback in the human drop is the compromise to the compartmentation principle. Many times, however, especially where the intermediary is a principal source, the human drop can be utilized to advantage. Barbers and bartenders are in excellent positions to serve in this capacity because both the investigator and the source have equal access to the intermediary.

The last communication means is the "pass." Here, quite simply, the source surreptitiously passes the message to the investigator. The pass could also be a key to a safety deposit box where the information has been placed for the investigator. This technique is usually accomplished on a busy street or in a crowded store where the brief contact between the source and investigator is not likely to be observed.

The proper method of communication will always be determined by the element of risk presented by the circumstances of the situation. Whatever technique the investigator decides upon, the communication aspect of the operation should be well planned and arranged prior to any operational activity.

8. Opposition

The opposition is the drug trafficking organization and includes all those who directly or indirectly assist the traffickers in the accomplishment of their objectives. The neighbor who alerts the trafficker to police surveillance, the bank official who warns the trafficker of official interest in his accounts, the telephone company employee who advises the trafficker of official telephone intercept activity; all these are examples of direct or indirect assistance. These individuals must therefore be considered as part of the opposition *

There are fundamentally two types of opposition. The first is what is known as "formal opposition." This consists of governments and/or government agencies which provide aide to the traffickers. There are several examples where national policy or widespread corruption has caused certain governments or official bodies of those governments to directly support drug trafficking activity.

The second type of opposition is commonly referred to as "informal" and includes the traffickers and anyone else associated with them who is not controlled or supported by an official organization.

In an effort to further their aims, the opposition will employ a variety of tactics against the investigating agency. The first of these is known as "provocation." A provocation is an act which is designed to elicit a certain action on the part of the investigator. The objective for the trafficker is to cause the investigator to waste time and resources in following false leads or misleading information. The trafficker may provide the investigator with information, through a member of the trafficking group posing as an informant, which will cause the investigator to concentrate his attention in one direction while the trafficker conducts his activity elsewhere. The false information can also lead to action by the investigator which will prove to be embarrassing to the agency. The main idea of a provocation is the deliberate provision of misleading information for some designed purpose, geared toward the benefit of the trafficker.

The second type of opposition tactic is the "penetration." This is the infiltration of the investigative agency by a member of the opposition. In the example provided above, the opposition member, posing as a source or informant, first penetrates the agency by establishing a relationship with an investigator. The penetration then facilitates further opposition action against the investigation, as well as providing the opposition with an opportunity to do some intelligence collection activity of their own concerning the activities of the agency, A penetration may be said to be the standard undercover operation, conducted in this case by the trafficking organization.

The next tactic is known as "monitoring" or, more commonly, counter surveillance. It consists of surveillance of the investigative agency's activities by the opposition. While this concept seems very fundamental, it is surprising to see how many agencies and investigators discount this possibility. Unfortunately, many times investigators underestimate the opposition's sophistication and resources and take for granted that this sort of activity does not take place. There are numerous examples of investigations being compromised and source's lives being endangered through failure to consider the possibility of opposition surveillance activity against the investigation.

The last type of opposition tactic is known as "negation." This is where the opposition uses a variety of techniques; e.g., political pressure, newspaper or magazine articles, allegations of corruption or civil rights violations, to damage or prejudice the agency's reputation or ongoing programs. The result of this damage will make it more difficult for the agency to call upon public and private support for its activities and thereby make it less effective.

9. Cover Measures

In the conduct of intelligence collection, it is necessary to disguise the effort in order to prevent the opposition from becoming are of the ongoing investigation. To avoid compromise cover are required, there are four basic types of cover which are utilized.

The first type is the "cover for status." ais cover provides the investigator or source with a role situation compatible with the requisite access to either the target or certain information concerning the target. For example, in an investigation concerning money laundering, a good cover for status would be that of a bank vice-president or a stock broker.

The second type of cover is known as "cover for action." This provides a plausible reason for the investigator or source to be conducting a certain action or to be in a certain area. For example, in order to conduct discrete surveillance of activity around a warehouse at a pier or airport, the investigator or source could take the role of cargo handler. Then if challenged the individual can provide a reasonable explanation for his presence without arousing too much suspicion. Cover for action is the type of cover most often used.

The third type of cover is "light cover." This is cover which is developed for short term utilization. It will not stand up to in depth scrutiny by the opposition. For example, if the investigator is detected examining a building, he can claim to be a real estate appraiser or some similar ruse. This may be adequate to allow the investigator to depart the area without arousing too much suspicion. This type of cover is usually not reinforced with false documentation.

The last type of cover situation is the "deep cover" operation where the investigator or source will be in a particular role with frequent contact with the opposition over a long period of time. An example of this type of situation is the sting operation. The agency can place undercover agents in a false company and offer to launder funds for narcotics traffickers. These agents will not go to their official office but will operate as if they are actually in some financial business. They may even take business trips, etc. with the traffickers. Usually this is a costly effort and is most often employed against high level targets where the result of the operation justifies the time and expense involved.

Where deep cover investigations are initiated, adequate steps must be taken to obtain the necessary "backs-topping . " Backstopping refers to the acquisition of all necessary materials to support a cover situation. In the example used above it would be necessary to rent office space, open commercial accounts , establish credit ratings, get letterhead paper, and do whatever else was required to sustain an inquiry by the opposition.
It is important to devote the proper attention to these details in order to avoid the possibility of compromise which could prove very dangerous to the undercover operatives.

As previously mentioned, these types of investigations are costly, especially where a deep cover situation is called for. Often times a considerable amount of time, effort, and expense is conserved by recruiting a source who has natural cover. If a legitimate bank official can be recruited to provide access to the trafficker's financial transactions, then it non-necessitates the establishment of a complex cover situation. The benefits of this situation are obvious, although some assurances will have to be provided to the bank official for protection against possible reprisal by the opposition. These kinds of details should be worked out in advance.

When sources are involved in the actual process of the collection of information, it will be necessary for them to store that information jn some form until it can be passed to the investigator. In sane cases, sources are located some distance from the investigator. Sore are inside the trafficker's organization where frequent communication with the investigator is extremely difficult. It is not advisable to have sources commit information to memory as details will inevitably be lost with the passage of time. It must be recognized that unless sore form of concealment plan, designed to prevent accidental discovery of the intelligence by the opposition, is devised and agreed upon, the source will always be at considerable risk. The investigator has the responsibility to insure that all sources are aware of the absolute need for the safeguarding of their collected information. The investigator must be certain that every source has developed some plan to adequately conceal the intelligence that the source has in his or her possession.

Many times the easiest form of concealment is a simple code system devised by the source himself. The investigator should be briefed on this code system so that the investigator will also be able to decipher the information should it become necessary. The important point to remember is that whatever system the source feels comfortable with and is adequate from the standpoint of security is acceptable. The investigator's primary responsibility is to make certain that the source has equipped himself with some concealment technique prior to actually commencing his or her activities.

11. Security

Security of the intelligence collection effort has been repeatedly stressed throughout this chapter. There are several different types of security. The first is "physical" security. This pertains to the security of the intelligence unit's location. The situation of the intelligence group should be such that access to this area is limited and controlled. It is not desirable to have the office located where the general public could easily wonder in and out. Some consideration should be given to whether or not open access should be available to other police officers and investigators not actually assigned to the intelligence unit. The possibility of penetration by the opposition is a constant risk. The area should be restricted to only those individuals who have a distinct need to be there and have the proper clearance. Sources should definitely not come to the intelligence office. For one thing the principle of compartmentation would be totally compromised. For another, the source could be identified through surveillance of the office by the opposition. Sources should always be contacted in safe areas away from the agency's facilities.

The second type of security is "personal" security or that necessary to protect the identity of the source or the investigator. This would include the use of code names for sources in written memoranda and the confidentiality of any files or documents containing sources' identities. It also involves the intelligence investigators maintaining a low profile to avoid drawing undue attention to their activities. Adequate backs-topping provides support for cover roles which enhances personal security. If the investigator does become known to the opposition he must be doubly cautious. One interesting technique in this circumstance has the identified investigator allowing himself to be observed in an apparent, amiable encounter with a member of the opposition. Actually, no relationship exists between them. This is a provocation action by the investigator whose intent is to cause suspicion amongst the traffickers about members of their own group. The final type of security is "operational" security which pertains to the conduct of the everyday operation of the intelligence unit. All investigative files should be kept in safes or locked cabinets. The intelligence group area should have an alarm system to prevent unauthorized entry if no one is there. Access to files should be restricted to only those individuals with a need to know. Investigators should be careful when discussing official matters outside of the office to prevent the possibility of being overheard.

All security considerations must constantly involve a balancing act between security and efficiency. If there is too much security, nothing can be accomplished. If there is too little, the probability of compromise is great. Those individuals responsible for managing intelligence collection operations need to continually review this area and make whatever adjustments are necessary.

12. Tools of the Trade

The tools of the intelligence trade are similar or identical to those utilized by any investigator. Casing is the first tool. This consists of the investigator viewing, investigating and evaluating every facet of an intelligence collection effort prior to taking any concrete action. For example, if. a site is proposed by a source as a convenient contact point, the investigator will first case it or check it out thoroughly. This process helps to prevent those errors caused by impulsive actions.

Another common tool is surveillance. All intelligence operations utilize surveillance as part of the overall effort. There is offensive surveillance which is the observation of the trafficker's activities by resources of the investigator. Counter-surveillance is the observation of the official agency and its activities by the opposition. Defense surveillance is the effort made by the investigator or a source to determine if he or she is being watched by the opposition. It is a very common error to discount the possibility of counter-surveillance. Every investigator should develop a series of traps; e.g., one way streets, dead end roads, blind alleys, etc., which can reveal the presence of counter-surveillance. These traps should be used on a regular but unpredictable basis. The convoy method has one investigator discreetly following another in order to observe any undue or continual interest in the activities of the first investigator by outside parties.

Another investigative tool employed is the conversational arts. Interviewing techniques are practiced with subjects who are willing to assist the investigation by providing information. Interrogation techniques are used against hostile or recalcitrant subjects.

Elicitation is often used in normal conversation where the subject is encouraged to speak. Once talking, the investigator listens enthusiastically, periodically stimulating the subject to continue. Many times the subject reveals far more than he had intended to. An example of this would be a supposedly casual conversation in a bar where the subject is unaware of the investigator's true identity. Technical devices are also used as part of the investigator's arsenal of investigative tools. These include electronic listening devices, such as concealed body transmitters, room bugs and telephone interception equipment. Electronic viewing devices, such as video cameras and night scopes, can also be used. Centralized records are generally an indication of an intelligence unit's level of sophistication and provide another tool. The collection of information in an orderly manner with some logical filing system provides access for future reference and insures that the intelligence collected will not be wasted or lost in subsequent investigations. These centralized records need to be secure against unauthorized entry.

SUMMARY

The reasoning behind the emphasis on intelligence collection should be clear. Law enforcement authorities are constantly tasked with increasingly sophisticated types of activities. Among these are the in depth long term investigative effort geared to provide information concerning top level, international narcotics traffickers. This information is necessary for successful interdiction and immobilization.

It is only through a well-planned intelligence collection program that law enforcement can reasonably expect satisfactory levels of success.

Simply making routine arrests and seizures is not sufficient to seriously impact the major targets. It is through the creation of fully professional intelligence gathering operations that the best results, in terms of seriously damaging the narcotics traffic are obtainable. The application of the twelve principles described above will greatly enhance the professionalism of the intelligence collection effort.

PERSONAL HISTORY REPORT	1. FILE NO. SOT-85-0016	2. G-DEP IDENTIFIER

3. SUBMITTED AS (Check applicable boxes)

- [ ] G-DEP SUBMISSION
  - [ ] INITIAL
  - [ ] SUPPLEMENTAL
- [ ] ARREST
  - [ ] INITIAL
  - [ ] FUGITIVE
- [X] INFORMANT ESTABLISHMENT
  - [ ] REGULAR
  - [X] RESTRICTED-USE
  - [ ] DEFENDANT
  - [ ] FOREIGN - REGISTERED
- [ ] FUGITIVE DECLARATION

4. FILE TITLE

COOPERATING INDIVIDUAL

5. DATE PREPARED 1/30/85

6. NAME (Last, First, Middle: Title, i.e., Capt., Dr., etc.)
Jones, John Thomas

7. NADDIS NUMBER 1234576 or Naddis Negative

9. ADDRESS (No., Street, City, State, ZIP Code)
16 1040 Jackson Ave., Brunswick, GA 31520

8. ALIAS OR OTHER NAMES

10. PHONE NO. (Include Area Code) (912) 555-2640

11. CHINESE TELEGRAPHIC NAME CODE N/A

Slim/Johnny

12. DATE OF BIRTH (Mo., Day, Yr.) /30/47

13. PLACE OF BIRTH (City and State) Charleston, SC

14. CITIZENSHIP U.S.

15. ILLEGAL ALIEN [ ] Yes [X] No

16. NATIONAL ORIGIN American

17. RACE W

18. SEX [X] M [ ] F

19. HEIGHT 6'0"

20. WEIGHT 170 lbs.

21. EYES Brown

22. HAIR Black

23. IDENTIFYING CHARACTERISTICS (Scars, Marks, Physical Defects, etc.)
1 inch scar over right eye

24. OCCUPATION
- [ ] Merchant Seamen
- [ ] Air Crewmen/Pilot
- [X] Other (specify) owner/operator Jones, Liquors

CG / FAA Number

25. SOCIAL SECURITY NO. 86-30-2788

26. FBI NO. None

27. DEA REGISTRATION NO. N/A

28. OTHER NOS. (Federal, State, Local) NIIS #1678094

29. PASSPORT NO. 2156784

30. VISA APL. NO. N/A

31. ISSUING COUNTRY U.S.

32. NAME ON PASSPORT John Thomas Jones

33. DRIVER'S LICENSE

a. State or Country	b. Number	c. Expiration Date
A	2043628	3/30/88

34. VEHICLE REGISTRATION

a. Make	b. Year of Vehicle
Toyota	1983
c. License No. 817-Van	d. Year 1985	e. State GA

35. CASE CLASSIFICATION IS BASED ON THIS SUBJECT? [ ] YES [ ] NO

36. CLASS OF VIOLATOR (Check one) [ ] 1 [ ] 2 [ ] 3 [ ] 4
Classified Under Drug Code.

37. FILE REFERENCES (G-DEP ONLY)

CRITERIA IDENTIFICATION
Quantitative (Enter Numeral) [f] [g] [h] [i]
Qualitative (Enter Letter) [ ]

38. LOCATIONS OF CRIMINAL ACTIVITY (City, State, Country)
Brunswick, GA

40a. CRIMINAL ASSOCIATES (Last, First, Name)

40b. NADDIS NO.

40c. SOURCE OF SUPPLY (Name)
James David Hardin

40d. NADDIS NO. 8671

41. PRIOR CRIMINAL RECORD
1983, GBI, Brunswick, GA, Poss. of handgun sent 2 yrs. Prob. (or pending charge)

42. DATE OF ARREST	43. PLACE OF ARREST (City and State)	44 ARMED [ ] Yes [ ] No

	Yes	No	46. DATE	47. AGENCY RELEASED TO	48a. TYPE OF VIOLATION (Possession, Sale, etc.)
Released to other agency					
Prosecution authorized			50. DATE	51. JUDICIAL DISTRICT	48b. MAJOR DRUG, Violator was Charged With (Heroin, cocaine, etc.)
Magistrate Hearing: Bound Over			53. DATE	54. BAIL AMOUNT $	55. BAIL POSTED [ ] Yes [ ] No / 56. PERSONAL RECOGNIZANCE [ ] Yes [ ] No

57. & 57b. CHECK BOXES) ONLY IF INFORMATION VOLUNTARILY SUPPLIED BY SUBJECT IN ITEM 6 ABOVE -- Privacy Act Requirement.

a. IMMEDIATE FAMILY (Last, First, Middle Name)

b. ADDRESS (No., Street, City, State, ZIP Code)

Spouse: Jones, Maryann (Jacobs) — [ ] 1040 Jackson Ave., #16, Brunswick, GA 31520

Father: Jones, James Melvin — [ ] 1560 Woods Place, Charleston, SC

Mother: Williams, Cynthia Ann — [ ] 464 E. Tremono, #7, Bronx, NY 10496

Form - 202 1985

Previous edition dated 8/84 may be used until supply is exhausted.

Exhibit 1

Exhibit 1

58. REMARKS *(Refer to Item No. when applicable)*   Page 2

Item 57a (Cont'd.)   Sister: Sizzler, Jo Beth   111 W. 112th Street
                                                     #8B, New York, New York

Jones was cautioned/advised per DEA Agent's Manual, 6612.31F:

(1) Must not violate any criminal law in furtherance of gathering information or
    providing services to DEA and that any evidence of such violation will be
    reported to the appropriate agency.

(2) He has no official status as agent or employee of DEA.

(3) The information Jones provides may be used in a criminal proceeding and even though
    DEA will use all lawful means to protect his confidentiality, that cannot be
    guaranteed.

Jones is a close associate and trusted friend of James David HARDING, a documented
HEROIN violator in the Brunswick, GA area. During the past several years, Jones
worked as a HEROIN distributor for HARDING. Jones will be utilized by DEA to
provide intelligence information on HARDING'S HEROIN trafficking operation and to
introduce an undercover agent to HARDING for the purpose of purchasing HEROIN.

Jones is a "restricted-use informant" in that Jones is currently on Georgia State
Probation for possession of a weapon. On 1/30/85, S/A Ackerman spoke, telephonically,
with Mr. John Doe, Jones' GA state probation officer (912) 555-4870 regarding Jones.
Mr. Doe gave verbal approval to S/A Ackerman for the utilization of Jones. Mr. Doe
requested that S/A Ackerman inform Jones that Jones will continue meeting with
Mr. Doe for the scheduled probation appointments. Mr. Doe is forwarding written
approval for DEA's utilization of Jones.

Jones was not made any promises or assurances regarding his legal situation
other than Mr. Doe will be made aware of Jones' cooperation.

No promises of rewards neither, monetary or nonmonetary were made.

NCIC records show that Jones is not wanted by any law enforcement agency. Glynn
County and Brunswick Police Department records show there are no outstanding
warrants for Jones.

(SEE 6612.27 6612.31)

58. AGENT'S NAME *(Print or Type)*	59. AGENT'S SIGNATURE	61. DATE
Willie Ackerman, S/A	/s/ Willie Ackerman	1/30/85
62. SUPERVISOR'S NAME *(Print or Type)*	63. SUPERVISOR'S SIGNATURE	64. DATE
Frank Jackson, G/S	/s/ Frank Jackson, G/S	1/30/85

SAC APPROVAL *(If appropriate)*

65. REVIEWED BY	66. CONCURRENCE	67. DATE
H. Warren Anderson, SAC	☒ Yes ☐ No	1/30/85

HEADQUARTERS APPROVAL *(If appropriate)*

68. REVIEWED BY	69. Office Symbol	70. CONCURRENCE	71. DATE
		☐ Yes ☐ No	

☆ U.S. GOVERNMENT PRINTING OFFICE 1986 – 491-509/45700

Page 1

See Instructions on Reverse before completing.	VOUCHER FOR PAYMENT FOR INFORMATION AND PURCHASE OF EVIDENCE	Voucher No. _____ Schedule No. _____

1. Originating Office (Name and Office Designator)
Quantico D.O.
OT

2. Name of Claimant
S/A John Doe

3. Claimant Social Security No.
555-55-5555

4. This Voucher is being used for:

a. [X] Payment to Informant
- (1) [X] for Information and Expenses $500.00
- (2) [ ] for Reward $
- (3) [ ] for Security $
- (4) [ ] for Payment of Moiety Claim $

b. [ ] Purchase of Evidence $

PAID BY

5. EXPENDITURES

a. File Number(s)	b. Amount	c. G-DEP Identifier	d. Exhibit No.
OT-87-0001	$ 500.00	DA1-C1	
	$		
	$		

5a. Purchase of DRUG Evidence — Drug Code (See Reverse) — **OR** — **5b. NON-DRUG Evidence (Describe Purchase)**

Quantity (Same as DEA-7)

7. CERTIFICATION OF INFORMANT

I certify I received payment in the amount $500.00 dollars U.S. or the equivalent in another currency.

If funds received are for the purchase of evidence, any unused funds shall be returned to the Government upon demand and any misappropriation will render me liable for prosecution.

Informant Code No. OF1-87-001 _____ (Sign LAST COPY only) _____ Date _____

8. REMARKS:

See report by S/A John Doe dated 1/1/87 re: debriefing of, OF1-87-001.

9. CERTIFICATION

a. PAYOR NAME:
(Signature) _____ Date _____
(Type name) S/A John Doe

b. WITNESS NAME:
(Signature) _____ Date _____
(Type name) S/A Bill Smith

c. APPROVING SUPERVISOR NAME:
(Signature) _____ Date _____
(Type name) G/S Tom Jones

10. Approving Headquarters Official When Required

11. ACCOUNTING CLASSIFICATION

Appropriation	Allowance Center	B/A	Incurring Center	Control No.	Program	Project	Benefitting Center	Object Class	Amount

12. Signature of Authorized Certifying Officer _____ Date _____

13. Signature of Claimant _____ | **14. Date**

Imprest Fund

DEA Form - 103 (Aug. 1982)   Previous editions are Obsolete.

PERSONAL HISTORY REPORT

...........to an informant and not a voucher f - accounting purposes.

ems 7, 9a, and 9b must be completed at the actual time of payment to the informant. Item 9c may be completed subsequent to payment (but within hours). Items 1 through 6 may be completed either, prior or subsequent to actual payment.

em 1. Office Name and Designator. See Appendix 62A, e.g., Hartford Resident Office (CD). When the paying office differs from the establishing office, the paying office will keep the signed copy (copy 5) and forward reproduced copy to the establishing office. If such a payment is made at the request of the establishing office, the request shall be documented by teletype.

em 2. The claimant is the person who withdrew the funds from the imprest fund and is responsible for submission of the voucher for accounting.

om 3. Self-explanatory.

em 4. Use of Vouchers:

    a. (1) Use this line to reflect payments to an informant during an investigation.

    b. (2) Payment for reward is defined as payment made after an investigation has been concluded.

    (Remainder of Item 4a is self-explanatory.)

    b. Use this line to reflect amount either expended by undercover agent or advanced to informant for purchase of evidence.

    Note: Do not combine PE and PI payments on the same form.

n 5. All expenditures of PL/PE funds must be referenced to appropriate investigative files. For each file number in 5a, enter the amount in 5b and the assigned G-DEP identifier in 5c. When reporting a payment to an informant and a general file is identified in Item 5a, enter in Item 5c the first four characters of the G-DEP identifier best describing the payment. Then add a zero as the last digit, e.g., QA1-IM, QG1-CD, etc. Where the funds were expended for purchase of evidence, enter in 5d the appropriate exhibit number or letter.

1 6. Description of Evidence.

    a. When 5d is completed, enter in 6a the G-DEP drug code of the suspected drug in the block provided and the quantity from Item 10 of the DEA-7. Drug codes are:

A Amphetamines including Methamphetamines (Schedule III)	I Other Stimulants
	J Other Drugs
B Morphine Base	K Hashish
C Cocaine	L LSD
D Other Depressants	M Marihuana
E Opium	N Barbiturates (Schedule II)
F Methadone	O Hashish Oil
G Other Hallucinogens	P PCP
H Heroin	

    b. Self-explanatory.

7. The amount will be stated in U.S. dollars. If a foreign currency was paid or advanced, enter in remarks (Item 8) the name of the currency and the conversion rate on the date the currency was obtained. When the full amount advanced to an informant for the purchase of evidence is not expended, explain the disposition of the amount returned by the informant in remarks (Item 8).

8. See Item 7.

9. Certification of payment.

    a. The payor is the person who physically made the payment for the purpose checked in Item 4; the payor may or may not be the claimant, depending on the circumstances of payment.

    b. This item must be completed by a witness to the payment when funds are paid to an informant.

    c. This item will be completed by the supervisor approving a payment for purchase of evidence or to an informant. Where the supervisor is also the witness to the payment, he will sign on both lines 9b and 9c.

0. Where the payment being reported required Headquarters approval, the name of the approving Headquarters official and the date of the approval will be entered.

1. This item will be completed by the fiscal unit and will reflect the expenditures reported in Item 5.

12, 13, and 14. Self-explanatory.

PRIVACY ACT INFORMATION

AUTHORITY: Title 21, U.S.C., Section 006
PURPOSE: To provide for a written accounting of advanced funds.
ROUTINE USE: To report expenditure of advanced funds.
EFFECT: Failure to provide employee information required will normally result in the failure to clear the employee's account for advance of funds expended.

Exhibit 3

SOURCE DEBRIEFING GUIDE

The Drug Enforcement Administration's Office of Intelligence, Office of Enforcement, and Office of Science and Technology have prepared this SOURCE DEBRIEFING GUIDE to assist the investigator with his or her formulation of questions concerning the international and domestic drug traffic. It is intended to be a resource document to supplement the interrogative skills and knowledge of the investigator in the technical areas of drug production, processing, and distribution.

The Source Debriefing Guide sets forth what DEA needs to know about the drug traffic our requirements so that we can pursue our mission to significantly reduce this problem.

Each person to be interviewed or interrogated be he or she a defendant, suspect or witness will not normally be able to supply information on all aspects of the drug traffic. Accordingly, a series of GENERAL QUESTIONS is provided in Part I of this Guide designed to identify the areas of knowledge possessed by the person being questioned. It is recommended that all of the GENERAL QUESTIONS be asked of each person so that areas of knowledge not immediately obvious may be surfaced.

Part II of the Source Debriefing Guide consists of eight sections, each comprised of specific questions concerning areas of knowledge. By using the GENERAL QUESTIONS in Part I to identify the specific areas the subject is knowledgeable about, the investigator can refer to a specific set of questions on these areas in Part II.

In those areas where the subject has extensive and detailed knowledge of very technical matters, such as a chemist or other technician, it may be worthwhile to request technical debriefing assistance from expert DEA personnel or other appropriate sources.
Where such a request is considered, the specific questions in that section of Part II dealing with the subject's knowledge should be answered so that an initial evaluation of subject's value may be made.

Exhibit 3

Exhibit 3

INDEX TO SOURCE DEBRIEFING GUIDE

2

Exhibit 3

PART ONE

GENERAL QUESTIONS REGARDING DRUG TRAFFICKING

1. Which illegal narcotic, restricted or controlled drugs have you used, sold or transported? During what time period? Specify and explain:

- Heroin
- Cocaine
- Hashish
- Liquid hashish
- Marihuana
- Opium
- L.S.D.
- P.C.P.
- Amphetamine
- Barbiturates
- Other drugs (Specify)

2. Who is the source of supply? Where is this person located? Where did this person obtain the narcotic, restricted or controlled drugs? Who are the distributors of these drugs?

3. Who else is involved in the distribution system?

4. Do you have any knowledge of where these types of drugs are manufactured, processed or stored? (See Part Two, Sections I (A) and (B); See Part Two, Sections II (A) and (B).)

5. Do you have any knowledge of the smuggling of drugs across U.S. borders? If so, what are the entry points? (See Part Two, Sections I (C).)

6. Do you have any information regarding methods used to transport drugs? (See Part Two, Section IV.) Specify and explain:

- Automobile
- Truck   - private
- Camper Truck   - commercial
- Bus
- Airplane   - private
                         - commercial
- Boat   - private
                         - commercial
- Body Carry
- Concealment in   - luggage
                         - food
- Mail   - other containers
- Others   - explain

3

Exhibit 3

7. Describe the method of concealment, type of vehicle and persons involved. (See Part Two, Section IV.)

8. Who finances the drug trafficking operations? (See Part Two, Section VI and VIII.)

9. Are you aware of any other method of concealment and transportation of drugs? (See Part Two, Section IV.)

10. What is the purity of the drugs being smuggled into the United States? At the laboratory? At the U.S. Border? In the United States?

11. What is the cost of the drugs being smuggled into the United States?

12. Have you ever seen or been told about coca, marihuana plants or fields either in the United States or in a foreign country? (If answer is yes, see Part Two, Section I.)

13. Do you have any knowledge of a heroin, cocaine, restricted or controlled drug laboratory in the U.S. or in a foreign country? (If answer is yes, see Part Two, Sections I, II and III.)

14. How are the funds to pay for the drugs moved? (See Part Two, Section VI.) Specify and explain:

    - Cash
    - Money Order
    - Checks
    - Letters of Credit
    - Bank Deposits

15. Do you know the associates, businesses, or activities of other drug traffickers? (See Part Two, Section VIII.)

16. Do you have any knowledge of any other drug transaction?

17. Are you familiar with any other areas of the country or the world? Describe. Have you ever lived in the other areas? When? For how long?

18. Do you know of any other smuggling activity into or out of the United States? Are drugs exchanged for other smuggled goods?

19. Is there an exchange of one drug for another, for example, cocaine for heroin? Are arms being traded for narcotics? Identify the source of the arms or narcotics traded.

20. How are the drugs paid for? Money up front, or, are the drugs on consignment? Is payment in U.S. dollars or other currency?

4

Exhibit 3

21. Is there any official corruption involved in the activity? Who? Paid by whom? How much? For how long?

22. What is the principal ethnic group of the drug activity?

23. What languages do these people speak?

24. What special skills do they have?

25. Have you been involved in other non-drug criminal activity? Give the dates of involvement. Identify the crime category, the type of operation and the level of operation:

- Crime category   - sex, weapons, stolen property, robbery, arson, etc.
- Type of operation   - smuggling, fencing etc.
- Level of operation - organized crime, international, national, local etc.

26. Have you ever worked as a confidential informant? With what police department? Give dates and circumstances surrounding the case.

27. Have you ever been confined in a jail or prison or any other institution? Give names, dates, locations and circumstances.

5

Exhibit 3

PART TWO

QUESTIONS IN SPECIFIC AREAS OF DRUG TRAFFICKING

I. Production, Processing and Distribution of Opium-Heroin and Coca-Cocaine.

    (A) SOURCE

        1. Where are the opium, marihuana, or coca fields located? Indicate locations on a map, (1:250,000 or smaller scale).

        2. Identify the owners and cultivators of these fields, their residences and telephone numbers.

        3. When are the fields planted and when are they harvested?

        4. Are there any arrangements between the owner and the cultivators?

        5. Specify and explain the support for the fields:

            - Water sources   - Irrigation methods
            - Fertilizers   - Seeds
            - Financing arrangements   - How are the materials
                                       paid for?

        6. Are these fields protected? If so, by whom? Are the protectors armed? What type of arms? At harvest only or at other times?

        7. What yield is expected or obtained from these fields? (poppies, marihuana, coca) How many people are involved in preparing the field? Planting? Harvesting?

        8. Is the opium gum or coca paste stored in the fields, or is it moved? If moved, how, when, by whom and to whom?

        9. Do the local authorities know of these fields? Have the fields been previously destroyed by these officials? When? If not, why not? Identify "local authorities".

Exhibit 3

10. Are the same fields planted every year or are crops rotated?

11. Is double cropping practiced? (Illicit crops planted among licit crops.)

12. Are any other methods used to hide or disguise the fields?

13. Is the field protected by police, military or any other officials?

(B) HEROIN AND COCAINE LABORATORIES

1. Where are the laboratories located?

2. Are the laboratories located at the cultivation fields? If so, what type of processing is done?

3. Describe each laboratory operation. What amounts of raw material are used?

4. How is raw material obtained?

5. How can a laboratory be recognized from outside?

6. How was the equipment purchased? From whom?

7. Were "dummy corporations" etc., set up to cover these purchases? How was the equipment paid for (cash, check, bank drafts, electronic fund transfers)?

8. Where was the equipment delivered?

9. Were there any extra storage points or warehouses where equipment or supplies were stored before being brought to the laboratory?

10. How was broken eqipment disposed of?

11. Was any of the equipment repaired? By whom?

12. Was any of the equipment sold to other criminal elements or traded in toward the purchase of newer and/or bigger equipment?

13. Who installed the equipment?

14. Who provided the hook-ups for the utilities, ventilation, etc.?

7

Exhibit 3

15. What chemicals are used at the laboratory? Where are the chemicals obtained? Who supplies them? What equipment is used?

16. What manufacturers made the tablet presses? What models?

17. Were any modifications, such as different motors, made?

18. Who made the punches? How many punches were made?

19. What design was used for the tablet punches? Who provided the original design?

20. Who made the engineering drawings for the punches?

21. What manufacturing procedure was used to make the tablet punches? What cover story, if any, was used to explain the need for these tablet punches?

22. Describe the chemists. How and by whom are they trained? Do the chemists perform any other functions in the operation?

23. Who supplies the laboratory with operation money? How is money supplied - in local currency, U.S. dollars, bank drafts?

24. Is the laboratory protected from or by the police or military? If so, by whom? Are the guards armed?

25. Are there any electronic or manual alert devices used to protect the laboratory?

26. What yield is expected and obtained by the laboratory? How pure is the product?

27. Is the heroin or cocaine dyed or cut? With what?

28. Where are the diluents obtained?

29. Why are these diluents preferred?

30. What diluents would you substitute if these were unavailable?

31. Where is the finished product kept?

Exhibit 3

32. Does the laboratory operate continually? If not, when? Is the laboratory in operation only when an order is received or when a crop has been harvested?

33. How are the orders and instructions received or passed? Is there a telephone number or a contact point?

(C) TRANSPORTATION AND STORAGE IN COUNTRY OF MANUFACTURE

1. What type of transportation is used? What are the transportation routes?

2. How is the finished heroin or cocaine moved? Is it moved to another point, or does the buyer take possession of it at the laboratory?

3. How are the arrangements made to move, buy, sell or pay for the heroin or cocaine? In what currencies are payments made? What is the source of the payments?

4. What persons, groups, vehicles and buildings are involved? Who owns the vehicles or buildings?

5. How many people move the heroin or cocaine? Who are they?

6. Are special compartments used to conceal drugs in luggage, automobiles or aircrafts? Where are these prepared? Who makes them?

7. What transportation routes are used? Are the same ones used all the time? Who determines the transportation routes?

8. Are escort or convey vehicles used? Describe them.

9. Is the movement protected? How? How are these arrangements made?

10. Is the finished product moved to a location near a border point? If so, where? To whom?

11. Is the finished product kept near the laboratory? Where? Who keeps it? Who protects it?

9

Exhibit 3

(D)   IDENTIFICATION OF PERSONS INVOLVED IN TRANSPORTATION OF ILLICIT DRUGS

1.   What couriers do you know or know about?

2.   Who are the backers, financiers and protectors?

3.   Are there any other persons or groups involved?

4.   How are the couriers recruited?   How are they paid? Who does the recruiting?

5.   What are the ethnic origins of the couriers?   What are the ethnic origins of the backers, financiers and, protectors?

(E)   ARRANGEMENTS FOR OBTAINING OR MOVING THE DRUGS

1.   Specify the way arrangements are made:

      - Telephone
      - Cable
      - Written message
      - Other means

2.   Are controllers used to monitor the movement?   How do they get their instructions?

3.   How are high level couriers recruited and by whom?

4.   Are periodic reports made on the progress of the shipment?   If so, to whom and how?

5.   What ports or entry points are used for these shipments?   Why?

6.   What methods are used to conceal shipments?   Is smuggling involved?   Describe and explain.

7.   Are the shipments transferred inside a country to other means of concealment?   Describe.

8.   Are false documents involved in the shipments?

9.   How many people know when the shipments are coming and what methods are being used?   Identify them fully.

10.   Are any Customs, airport, airline or any other officials involved in these shipments?

Exhibit 3

11. How is the payment made, in advance or after receipt of a shipment? Explain.

12. Are the same people involved in the payment, as the movement, manufacture or sale of the shipment?

13. Identify any businesses or investments of the persons involved. (See Section VII.)

II.   Production, Processing and Distribution of Restricted and Controlled Drugs.

(A) SOURCE

1. What drug or drugs are involved? What form? What quantity?

2. What is the dosage form?

- White powder
- Capsules
- Pills
- Blotter
- Other, (Specify)

3. How are the drugs packaged?

4. Are you a courier? How are the arrangements made to pickup the drugs? Where do you stay?

5. Where do the drugs originate?

6. From whom and how are the drugs obtained? Is the supplier directly involved with the manufacturer?

7. What is the cost?

8. What is the cost of additional or lesser amounts of the drugs?

9. Where and to whom is it going? What were the delivery charges? What was the price of the drugs at the delivery site?

10. Give names and locations of people financing the operation. Do they handle any part of the shipment? Is anyone else involved in any way in this operation?

11

Exhibit 3

11. Do you know of a laboratory manufacturing or processing drugs? Do you know of any new processing techniques?

12. Have you ever seen any fields where drugs are being cultivated?

13. What methods are used to smuggle the drugs or chemicals? Describe.

14. Do you have any other knowledge concerning drugs, diluents or precursors used in making drugs?

(B)   ILLICIT LABORATORIES

1. How many people operate the laboratory? What are these people's names and addresses? Where are the laboratories located?

2. How often do the laboratories operate? 'Hours?

3. What type of equipment is in the laboratory? Describe in detail.

4. Are there any tableting machines? What type? What capacity? How many?

5. Describe any mixing equipment. What type and what capacity?

6. What manufacturing processes are used by the chemist?

7. What precursors are used? Where did they come from? How were they obtained? What methods were used to divert the drugs from the legitimate source? Give the names of the firms, country or origin and methods of operation, such as the use of brokers, false invoices, smuggling transhipments to other countries.

8. What packaging form is used? Describe. Where are the packaging materials obtained?

9. What equipment is used? Describe.

10. What diluents are used? Are the same ones always used?

Exhibit 3

11. Do you have or can you obtain samples for analysis?

12. To whom is the drug distributed after sale? In what form? What do they do with it? What points of smuggling are involved?

13. Do any of the suppliers or laboratories have any legitimate functions, such as manufacturing legal drugs? Are any of these drugs being diverted?

(C) DIVERSION OF LEGITIMATE DRUGS

1. How are the drugs obtained? By prescription from physicians? Over the counter from a druggist? Explain.

2. Are any records falsified by legitimate handlers to cover illegitimate distribution?

3. Are the drugs stolen? By whom, how, where and when? Give details.

4. How do you pay for the prescription?

5. How often can you get a prescription?

6. Does the physician perform a physical examination?

7. Does he know the drugs are not for legitimate use?

8. Will he sell numerous prescriptions or one prescription at a time? How large a volume will he prescribe or sell?

9. Does he use a fictitious name or his real name?

10. Does he identify the pharmacy where the prescription can be filled?

11. Is the pharmacist part of the scheme?

12. Is there a record covering the transaction?

13. If the physician sells directly, where are the drugs obtained?

14. Does the physician require a person to administer the drug in his presence?

Exhibit 3

15. What other types of drugs are available from the source?

16. Are the drugs sold by a pharmacist without a prescription? What volume? What price? What form?

17. Describe the labelling. Are the labels taken off or altered?

18. Does the pharmacist prepare a fictitious prescription to cover the transaction?

19. Dose he provide illegal refils of a legitimate prescription?

20. If the drugs were obtained from a wholesaler or manufacturer, at what point are they diverted?

21 Are the employees or the owners involved? Are both involved?

22. Is the diversion covered by falsifying records? If so, how is this done?

III. Questions for Persons with Detailed Knowledge of Laboratories.

(A) PRODUCTION

1. Where or from whom did you learn to make this drug? What is your educational background?

2. Where is or where was the laboratory located? What drugs are or were produced? Are or were there any other drugs produced?

3. Where are or were the chemicals and apparatus obtained?

4. Outline the synthetic procedure followed on a step by step basis. Are any written records kept? Where?

5. What scientific publications or journals were used in developing this synthetic procedure?

6. Wher did you obtain this procedure?

7. Estimate the time required for completion of each step?

14

Exhibit 3

8. How often does the laboratory operate? For how long?

9. How many different sites are used for production?

10. How are the wastes discarded? How is the laboratory ventilated? What steps are taken to ensure that vapors do not escape into the atmosphere where they might be detected? What security procedures are followed to avoid detection?

11. What are the sources of energy and water? Are they regular sources or are they furnished by irrigation?

12. What procedures, if any, are used to cheat or by-pass the meters on the utilities?

13. How much of the finished product is usually obtained per batch? How many batches are obtained per day, week or other applicable period?

14. How are the raw materials obtained, and from whom? How are they transported and received by the laboratory?

15. What quality control did products undergo, either in processing or when finished?

16. What safety precautions were taken to avoid hazards to health or property?

17. How many people were involved in the manufacturing operation? What were their duties?

18. How are laboratory personnel recruited? Trained? Retained?

19. If the operation is not year round, where do the laboratory personnel go during the "off season?" Other jobs? Other illicit duties?

(B) MARKETING

1. What records, if any, are kept? Can you obtain any?

2. How was the product packaged, shipped or stored?

3. To what extent do local marketing conditions dictate the use or modification of operating procedures? Example: Heroin that is produced in Southeast Asia is deliberately made fluffy because the manufacturers are paid in bulk rather than weight.

15

Exhibit 3

IV. Questions for Persons with Specific Knowledge of Smuggling or Transporting Drugs.

(A) SMUGGLING

1. Do you have direct knowledge of smuggling? If not, who told you about it?

2. What drugs, precursors or chemicals are being smuggled?

3. Where is the smuggling occurring? Give detailed locations. Identify transfer points, if any.

4. Who is involved? Is this person a runner for someone else? If so, for whom?

5. How is the smuggling done? Give details of any special devices or procedures used by the smuggler.

6. How often does the smuggling occur? Is there a set pattern?

7. Is any border official involved? Who? How is he paid off? By whom?

8. Who else knows about this smuggling?

9. When did you first learn about it? How long has it been going on?

10. Is there a fixed fee for smuggling? Is payment made in other contraband, merchandise or stolen goods?

(B) TRANSPORTATION/AUTOMOBILES

1. Are you aware of any pattern of transportation of drugs by car, truck or camper? Explain.

2. What type of drugs are being moved?

3. Who are involved? Identify the names, addresses, locations and associates.

4. What routes are used? Identify pickup points, transfer points, stash points and delivery points?

5. Has the vehicle been modified in any way to carry drugs? Explain.

16

Exhibit 3

6. Where and by whom are these modifications made? Does the vehicle modifier work for other groups?

7. How much is carried in each load? How often?

8. How long has this system been operating?

PRIVATE AIRPLANES

1. What types of drugs are being transported by private airplanes?

2. Who is the pilot? Does he own the plane? Is he a contract pilot? For whom?

3. Is the airplane rented? Borrowed? From whom? Is the owner knowledgeable about the purpose of the flight? Is he paid for the risk?

4. What is the make and color of the airplane? How many engines? What are the tail or wing numbers? Are registration numbers changed? How?

5. What quantity of drugs does each load consist of?

6. How often do they make their runs? Is there a pattern?

7. Does the airplane or ground crew have any special equipment? Is the landing area identified in a special way?

8. Where is the pickup point? Identify the location. Can you locate it on a map?

9. Where is the load delivered? To whom? What is the location?

10. Are the pilots or ground crews armed? What type of weapons?

11. What happens to the drug once it leaves the airplane? Identify and give licence numbers of vehicles that are involved. Identify ground crew and drivers.

12. What is the ultimate destination of the drugs? Who are the dealers involved?

13. Are there any special techniques used to avoid detection? Explain.

17.

Exhibit 3

14. Who owns or operates the field?

15. Is the field a commercial field? A private field? A clearer area specially prepared for smuggling?

COMMERCIAL AIRPLANES

1. What couriers are using commercial airlines to transport drugs? Identify by name and give description.

2. Are false passports used? Are false names and identifications used?

3. Identify airport and city at both departure and arrival points.

4. What type of drugs are transported? How many?

5. How are the drugs hidden, on passengers, in luggage or in the airplane? If in the airplane, how are they retrieved?

6. What is the frequency of the shipments? Is there a pattern?

7. Identify the person or group responsible for the shipment of the drugs. For whom are the drugs intended?

8. Describe any method known for shipping drugs in cargo.

9. Identify any airport or airline personnel involved.

10. How is the payment for airline tickets made? Cash, credit card or other methods?

11. Describe any special techniques used to avoid customs or airport security.

12. Are false documents used for shipping? Explain.

13. Are "controllers" used to surveil the courier at the airports or on the aircraft? Are signals used?

V. Persons Apprehended at a Border While Smuggling Contraband.

1. How may times have you crossed the border carrying contraband? Where, when, and with whom? What was the contraband?

Exhibit 3

2. What was the source of the contraband?

3. How much did it cost? How much were you paid? How much have you been paid in the past? From whom did you get your money? Where and when did you get paid?

4. How many accomplices do you have? Identify them. Are you under surveilance while carrying contraband?

5. Where is the contraband going?

6. How much will the contraband sell for?

7. Do you know anyone else involved in smuggling contraband across the border?

8. Describe any knowledge you have about the technique of concealing contraband.

9. Are you selling contraband of any kind? How much are you being paid? How much have you received in the past?.

VI. Persons Apprehended for Trafficking in Drugs.

1. From whom did you obtain your drugs? For whom are you selling drugs?

2. Where, when and in what place did you obtain the drugs?

3. Do you have more than one source of supply? From whom do you receive your supply? How many times have you received a supply from this person?

4. What do you pay for your supply? How much are you paid for your drugs?

5. To whom will you sell your drugs?

6. Does your source supply anyone else?

7. From where does your source obtain his drugs?

8. Where do they deliver it for your source?

9. How much does your source pay for it?

10. How did you get involved in selling drugs? How were you recruited? By whom?

19

Exhibit 3

PRIVATE BOATS AND SHIPS

1. Describe and identify any private boats used to transport drugs.

2. Who owns the boats? Where are they kept? Who are the crew members? Who is the major dealer involved?

3. What type of drugs are being transported? How many?

4. What ports, harbors, or marinas are used to load or unload the drugs?

5. What techniques are used to avoid detection? Does the boat have any other special equipment or hidden compartments?

6. How often is the boat used for drug deals? Is there any set pattern?

COMMERCIAL BOATS AND SHIPS

1. What commercial vessels are being used to transport drugs?

2. Are any officers or crew members of vessels involved? Identify.

3. Where are the drugs loaded and unloaded?

4. Are any false shipping documents used? Explain.

5. What special procedures and techniques are used to avoid detection during transportation, pickup and delivery?

6. What is the frequency of activity? Is there any set pattern?

7. Are there any customs or company officials or dock workers involved? Explain.

Exhibit 3

VII. Financial.

1. Does the subject derive any part of his income from illegal drug transactions?

2. If so, list all of the subject's assets (bank accounts, real estate, businesses, cars, etc.) aquired through his narcotics dealings.

3. What specific banks are used by the subject or members of his narcotics organization?

   (a) How often are transactions conducted at these specific banks?

   (b) Are these bank transactions drug-related?

   (c) If so, detail how the transactions (withdrawals, deposits, identity of depositors, etc.) are conducted.

4. Does subject have knowledge of any international transfer of funds by traffickers? If so, detail how the transfers are conducted.

5. What types of financial records or books are retained and where are they kept?

6. Does subject have knowledge of stocks, bonds, certificates of deposit (bearer) or businesses owned or in the possession of any individual connected to a narcotics organization?

7. Where are these or any other investments located?

8. If these investments are used to "wash" dollars, detail the methods used.

9. Do you have knowledge of other money-laundering techniques? Example: through casino profits?

10. Do you have knowledge of specific dates of bank transactions, drug sales and drug purchases by the subject? If so, state the dates and explain what occurred specifically on those dates.

21

Exhibit 3

VIII. Organized Crime

1. Are you involved in any capacity with organized crime?

2. Do you have any knowledge of anyone involved with organized crime?

3. What activity leads you to believe it is organized crime?

4. In what capacity is this involvement?

5. How long has this involvement existed?

6. If a member, who was the sponsor?

7. Is this involvement through a family or business relationship?

8. Through your association with organized crime, are you involved in drugs? Specify.

9. Besides drugs, what other activities do you have knowledge? (Activities such as arson, loansharking, and gambling are some of the most frequently encountered.)

10. Do you have access to any material implicating organized crime in these activities?

11. Where do you operate?

12. Where are some of the more frequently used meeting places?

13. To whom do you report?

14. Do you associate with members/associates of other groups?

15. Do you own, operate, or otherwise have an interest in any businesses? Specify.

16. Can you identify any businesses owned/financed by organized crime?

17. Do you have family or business associates outside the United States?

18. Can you identify other members or associates and their functions?

22

4 ANALYTICAL METHODS

MATRIX DEVELOPMENT AND LINK ANALYSIS

A great deal of raw information is collected during the course of significant, lengthy investigations. This information is then collated and placed in often complex and detailed written reports.

A basic goal for the analyst and investigator is to organize the information in such a way as to make the difficult task of analyzing the data easier.

The analysis techniques covered in this section are designed to place individual and organizational relationships in graphic formats that will aid in clarifying the respective relationships.

Many graphic forms can be developed to assist in this analysis. We will discuss but a few. These are merely tools, helping the analyst to form educated conclusions. They are not proposed as a panacea for the difficult job of information analysis.

The first tool, or technique, we will discuss is link analysis.
This involves the development of a network of links, or associations, in the form of a diagram. The interpretation of these diagrams is called Link Analysis.

LINK DIAGRAM

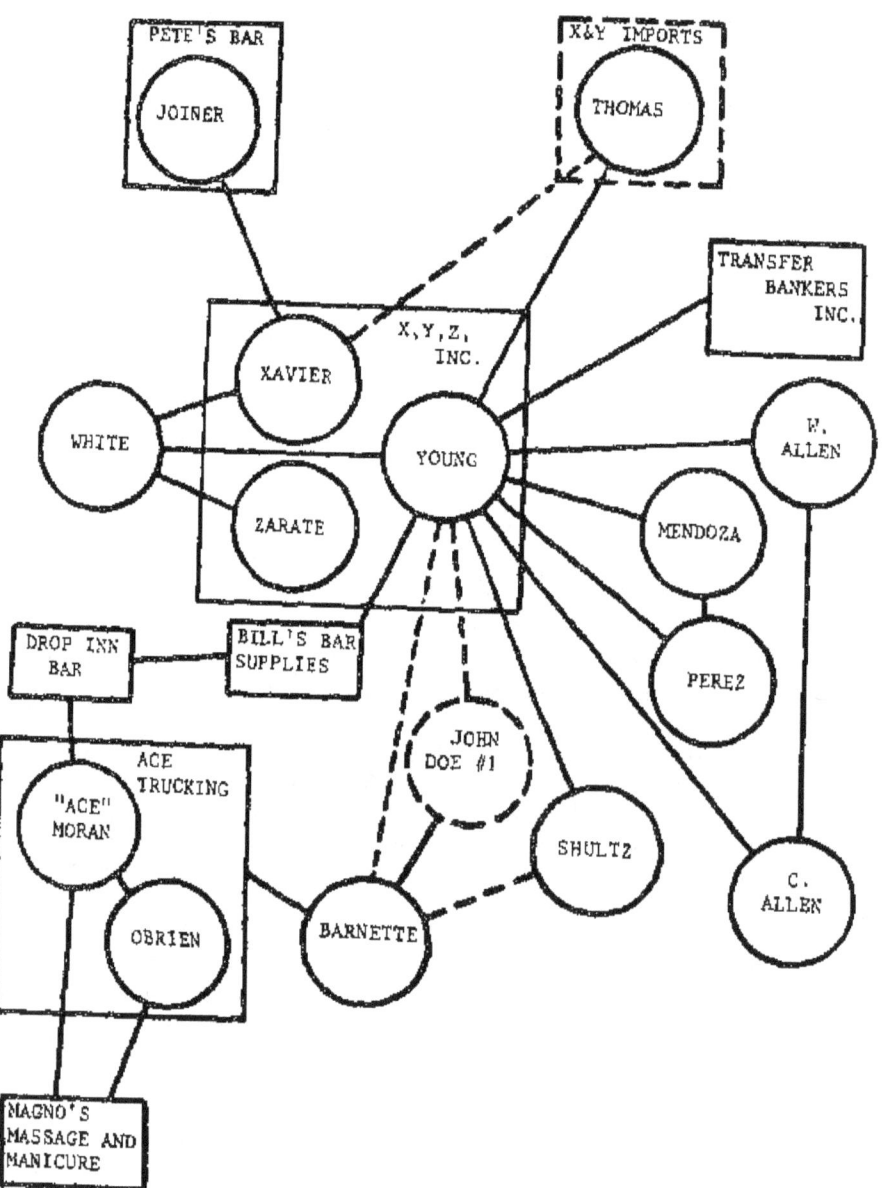

THE LINK DIAGRAM - PURPOSE

The link diagram provides the intelligence analyst with a visual model or representation of the associations between persons and/or organizations. The technique can also be adapted to show associations between telephone numbers, vehicular identification numbers, etc. At present, we will concentrate upon the associations between persons and organizations. Remember, an organization may be a business r club, or criminal coalition, etc.

THE EIGHT STEP SEQUENCE
The link diagram is constructed in an eight step process.

1. Assemble all Raw Data. The information must be organized (perhaps a summary, narrative report). Information comes from many sources and must be summarized to facilitate comprehension.

2. Select Names/Organizations of Importance. Highlight or Underline.

3. Construct the Association Matrix. Names and organizations must be alphabetized before the construction of the matrix. As an investigation continues, more and more entries will be placed on the matrix. Without alphabetical notation, significant entries could be lost.

EXAMPLE NO. 1

An association matrix is shown below. The association of distance between cities is demonstrated.

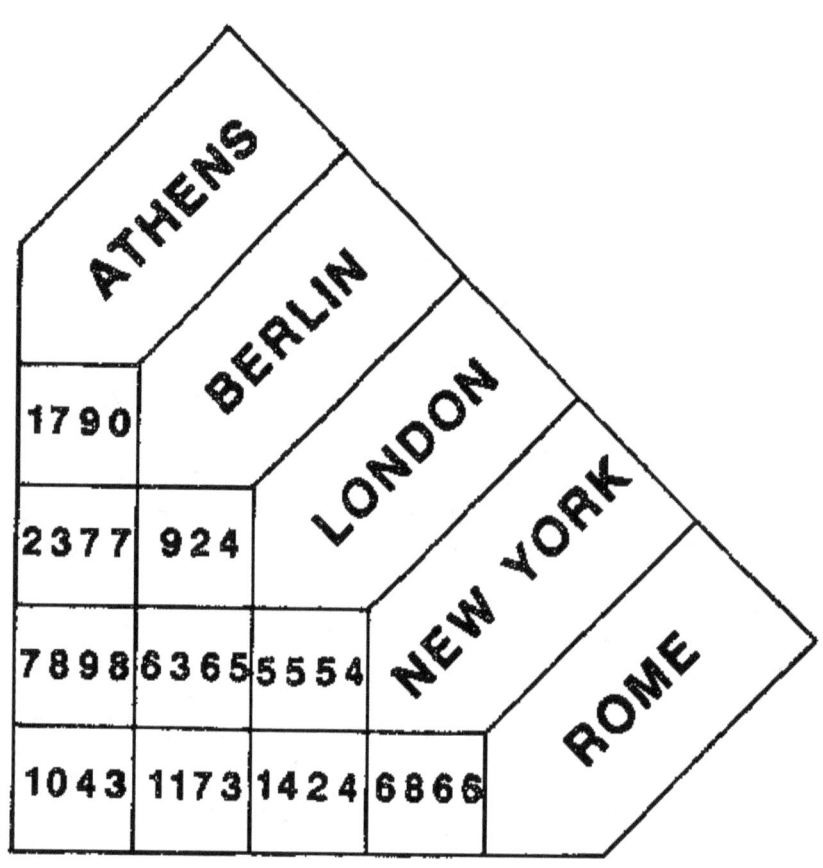

DISTANCE ASSOCIATION MATRIX

The cities distances are replaced by the names/organizations. The associated
Distances are replaced as described in the next step.

4. Enter the "Association" points in the matrix. Where there exists
association link between individuals, enter a large dot (.)
Where the association or link is weak, enter an open circle (o) .

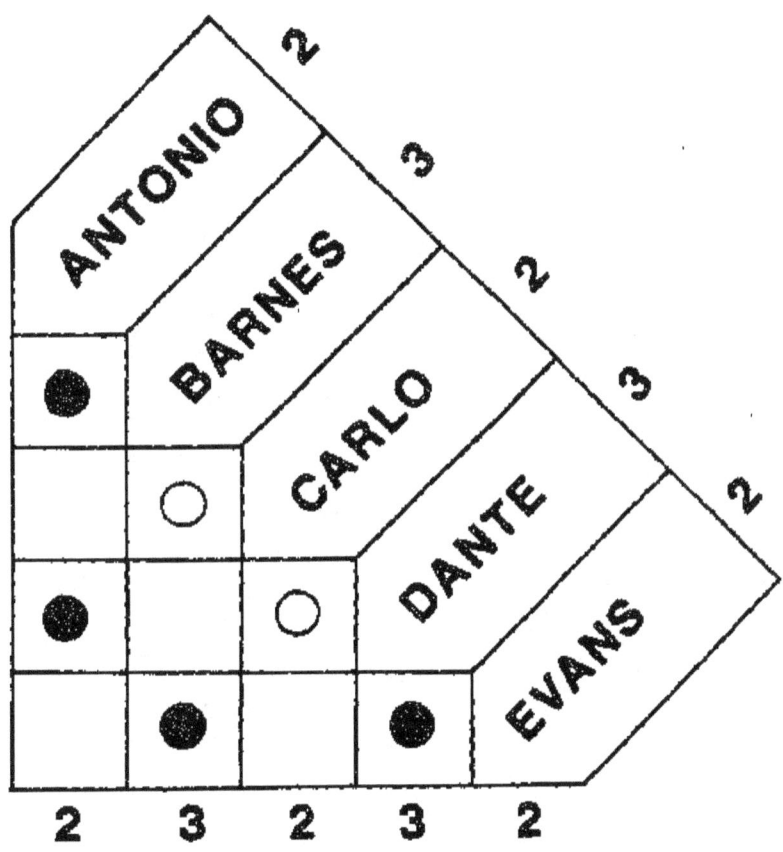

ASSOCIATION MATRIX

5- The association matrix is an interim step to the construction of the link diagram. A useful way to decide where to start the link diagram is to determine the number of links associated with each individual, whether weak or strong. The individual with the most links will be a useful starting point.

6 - Construct a Preliminary Diagram of the links between the individuals. Starting with the individual determined in Step 5, place the individuals on the diagram within individual "balloons". The individuals are "linked" by noting the associations shown in the association matrix with lines. Strong is shown by a solid line and the weak by a broken line.

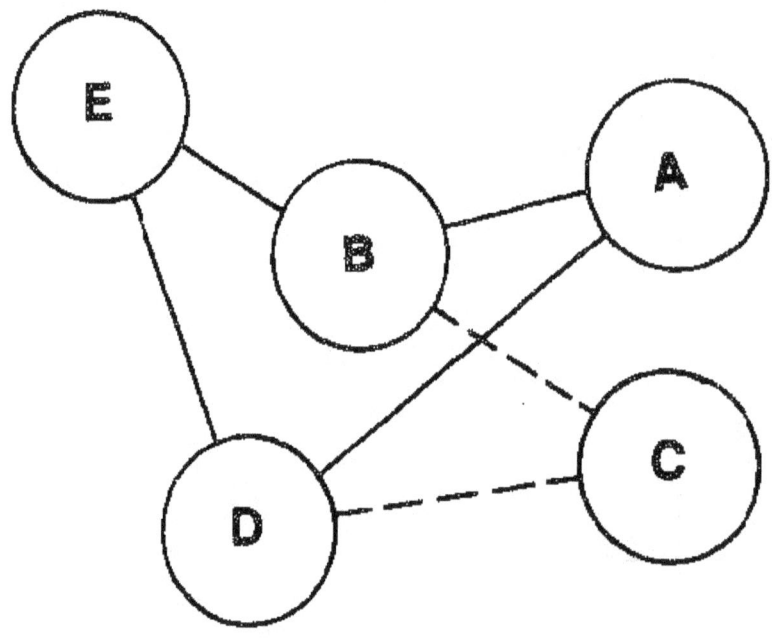

PRELIMINARY LINK DIAGRAM

7 - Clarify and Re-plot the diagram. Use straight lines and avoid having the lines cross. In more complex diagrams, this will simplify the analysis of the information demonstrated by the diagram.

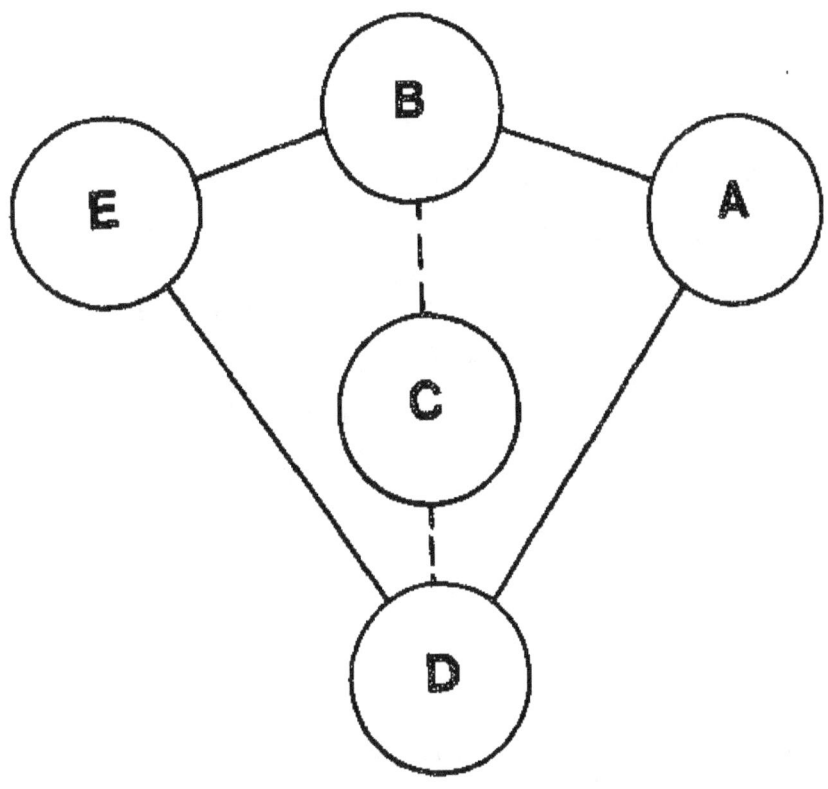

FINAL LINK

8 - Analyze the diagram. Remember, develop inferences.

Using the following scenario, we have constructed the ASSOCIATION MATRIX and
LINK DIAGRAMS as examples for the class exercises that will be presented.

1. BENITEZ AND OLIVARES ARE BUSINESS PARTERS.

2. BENITEZ HAS GIVEN LARGE QUANTITIES OF MONEY TO WANG.

3. HARDY IS THE OWNER OF A BUSINESS WHICH DEALS WITH THE BUSINESS OF BENITEZ AND OLIVARES.

4. DIOGARDI AND HARDY ARE OWNERS OF A VESSEL WHICH IS SUSPECTED TO BE USED FOR DRUG SMUGGLING.

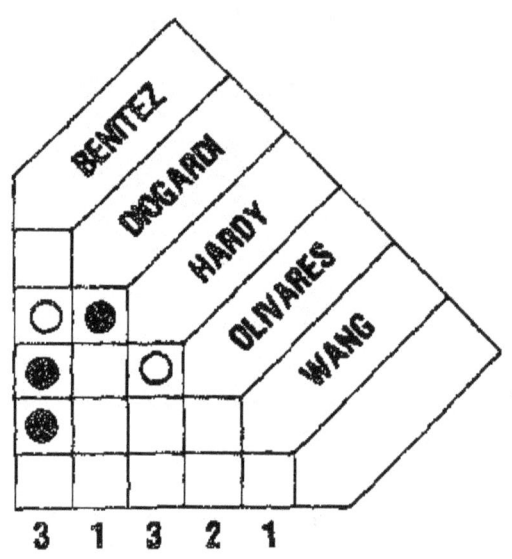

PRELIMINARY LINK DIAGRAM

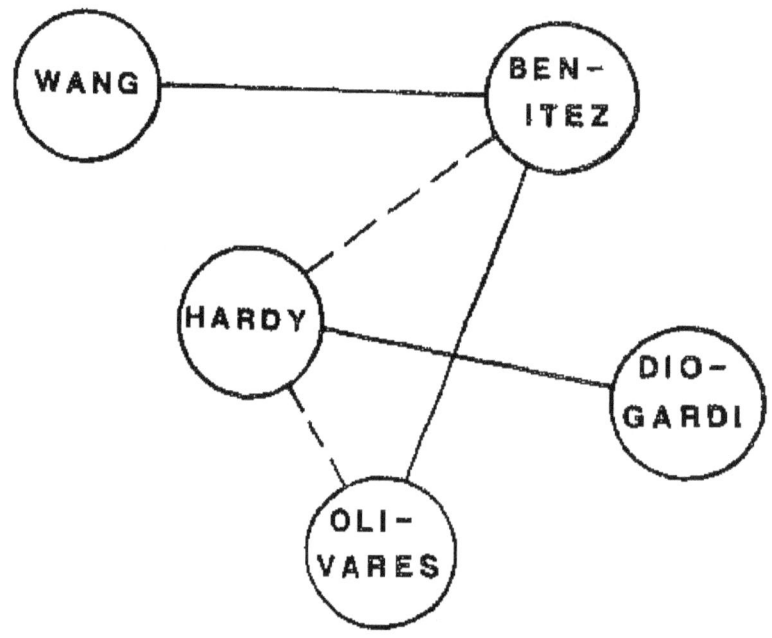

FINAL LINK DIAGRAM

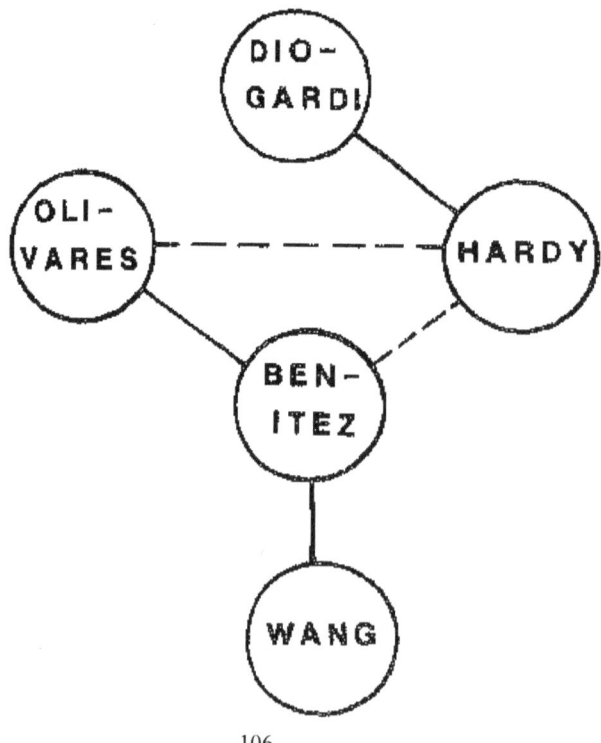

There are two methods of using an association matrix to show associations that exist between individuals, individuals and organizations, and organizations.

1. In the first, the association matrix relative to the individuals is developed as we have done previously. The organizations are then listed alphabetically, but separately from the individuals. The persons having membership in each organization are- then listed beneath that organization.

2. In the second method, list both the individuals and organizations in alphabetical order on the matrix. Enter the association points in the matrix diagram as before. Individuals may be associated with other individuals or organizations, for example; Mr. Rodriguez meets Mr, Mams and then visits the Martinez Travel Agency. Rodriguez is associated with Mams and the Martinez Travel Agency. Organizations may be associated, for example; telephone toll information reveals calls from unknown persons at the Martinez Travel Agency to Panama Red's Bar. Principals or individuals holding positions of influence over the operations of an organization are designated in the matrix by a plus {+) sign.

The associations and plus designations mav then be counted to establish the beginning point for the link diagram. It is suggested that for simplicity, the associations only be counted.

The individuals are again represented by circles. The organizations are denoted by squares or rectangles. Where individuals are principals of organizations their circles are enclosed by the organizational squares or rectangles.

EXAMPLE OF MATRIX AND LINK DIAGRAM SHOWING ASSOCIATIONS
BETWEEN INDIVIDUALS AND ORGANIZATIONS

1. Doyle and Harris are the owners of the Southern Automobile Agency.

2. Oliphant is the owner of the Golden River Motel.

3. Doyle is the President, and White is the Vice President of the Heller Moving Company.

4. Each week, White gives Barnes a package.

5. Harris services Oliphant's automobile.

6. Barnes receives money from Oliphant at the end of each month.

7. Harris and Barnes serve on the same committee of the Rotary Club.

SOUTHERN AUTOMOBILE AGENCY
DOYLE
HARRIS

GOLDEN RIVER HOTEL
OLIPHANT

HELLER MOVING COMPANY
DOYLE
WHITE

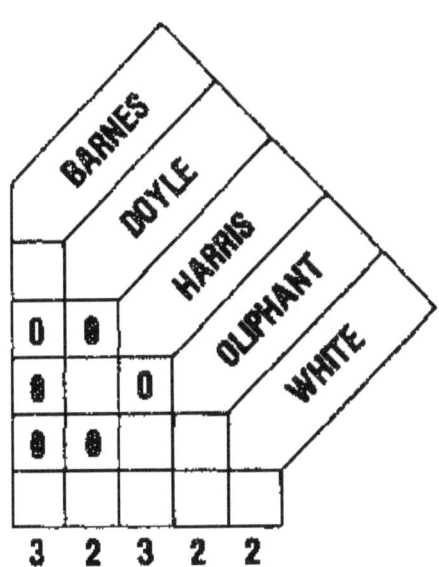

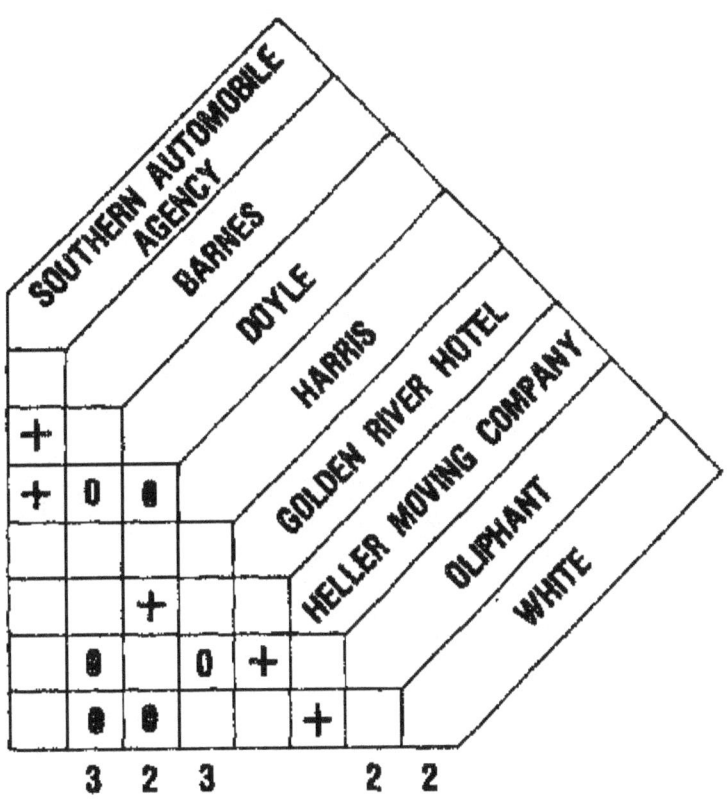

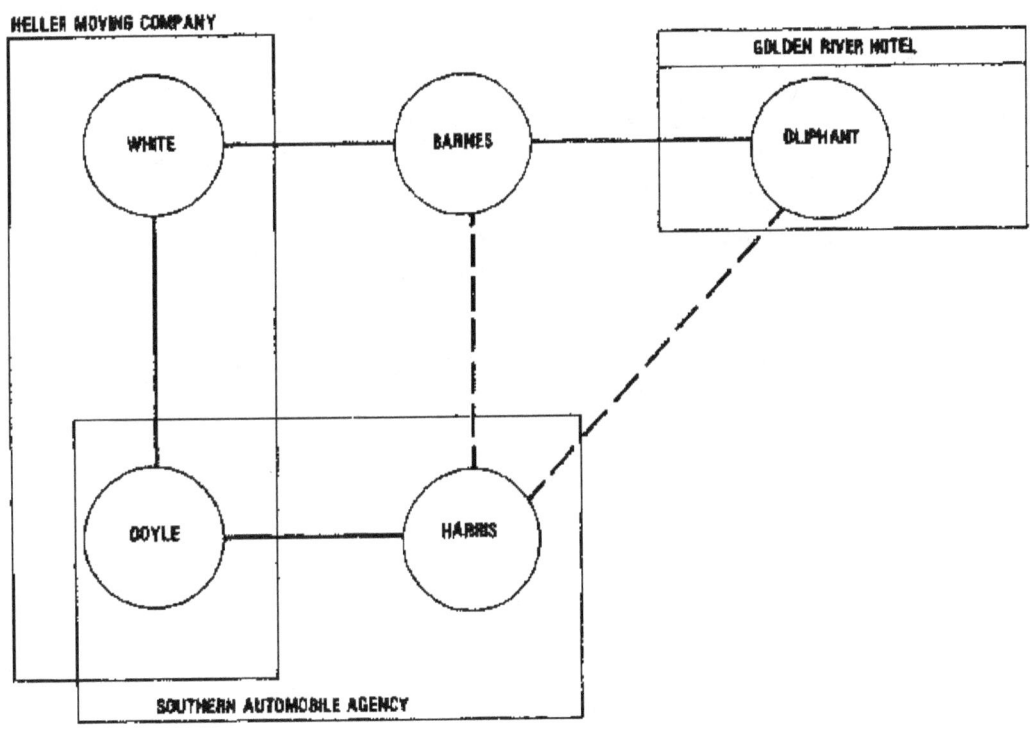

DIAGRAM OF ASSOCIATIONS BETWEEN INDIVIDUALS AND ORGANIZATIONS

NOTE: More complex associations among individuals and/or organizations may require different graphic representations. Some options for the more complex associations are the following:

INDIVIDUALS WITH MEMBERSHIP IN MORE THAN ONE BUSINESS OR ORGANIZATION

EXAMPLE: Joseph Murphy is the Director of White Sales Co. and Chairman of B.A. Sullivan and Sons Memorials.

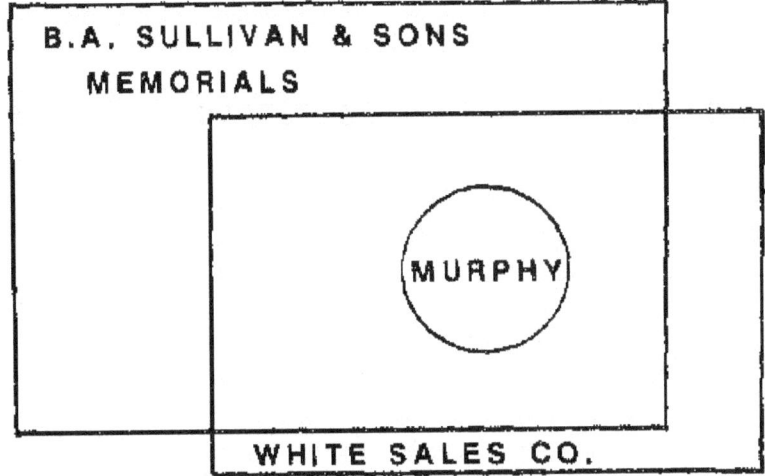

MEMBERSHIP IN TWO ORGANIZATIONS

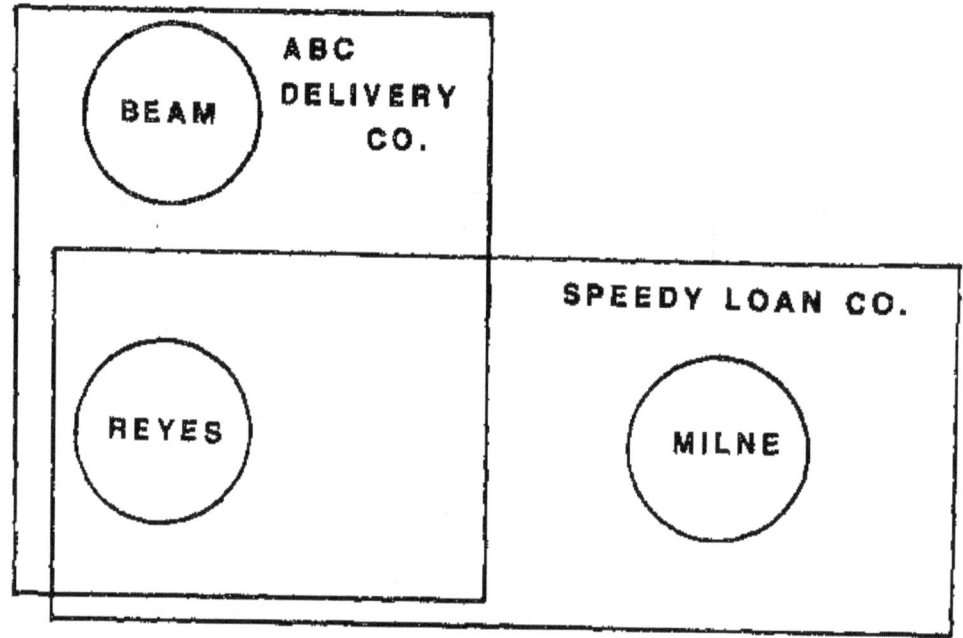

MEMBERSHIP IN THREE ORGANIZATIONS

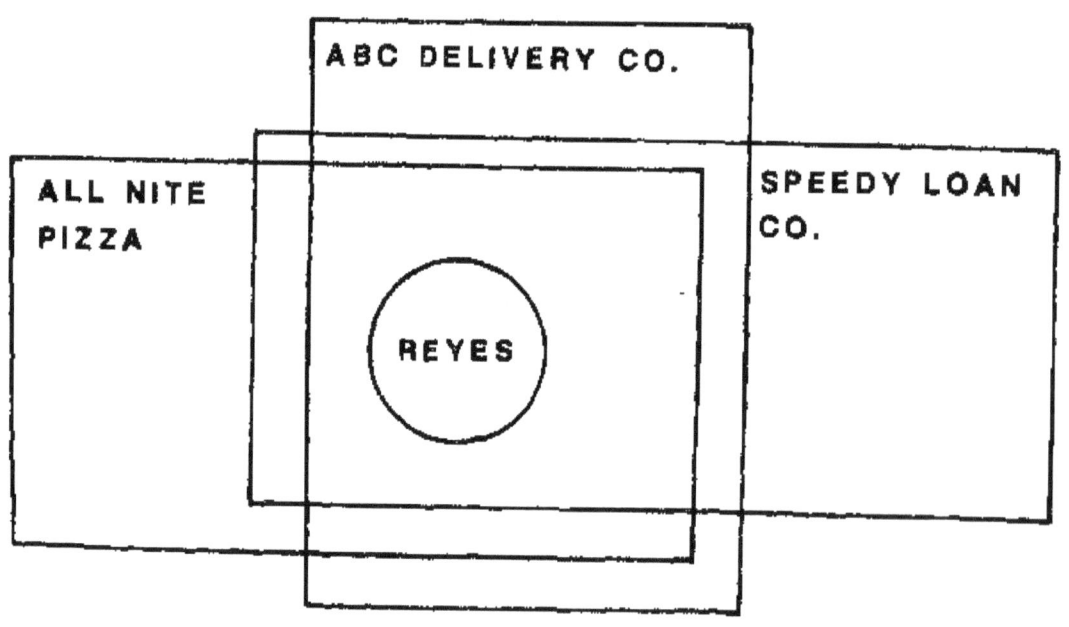

INDIVIDUAL WITH MEMBERSHIP IN NUMEROUS ORGANIZATIONS

ASSOCIATION BETWEEN INDIVIDUALS WITHIN SAME ORGANIZATION

INTERNAL LINKS SHOWN

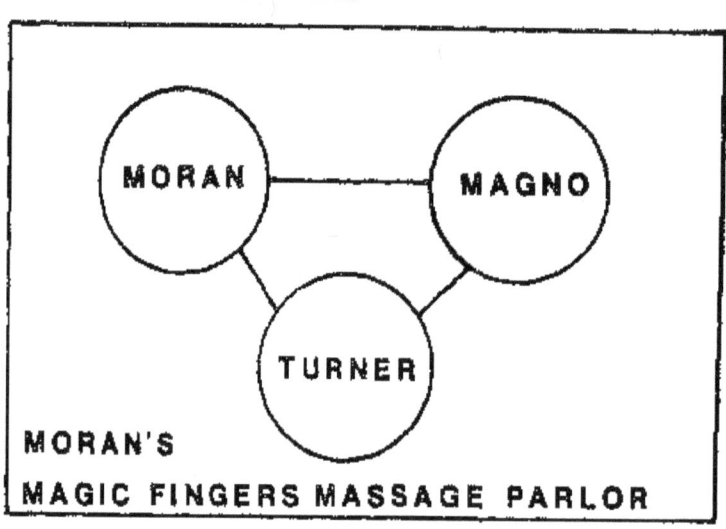

INTERNAL LINKS INFERRED

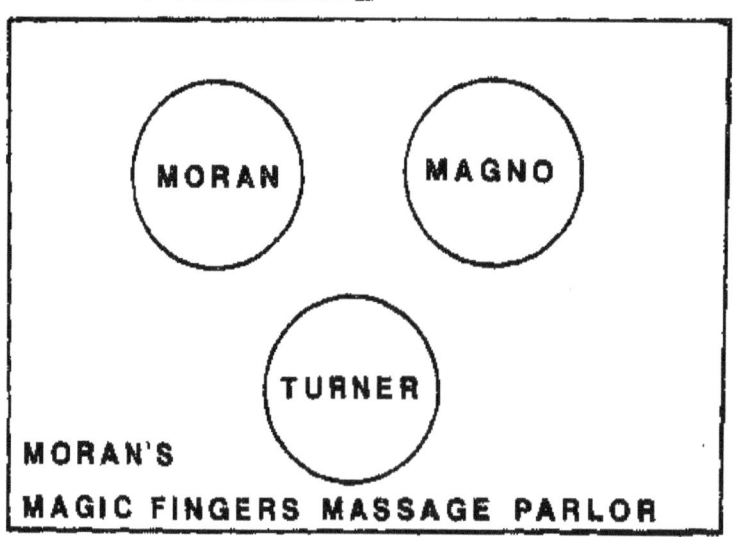

<u>ASSOCIATION BETWEEN AN INDIVIDUAL AND AN ORGANIZATION</u>

(INDIVIDUAL LINK NOT KNOWN)

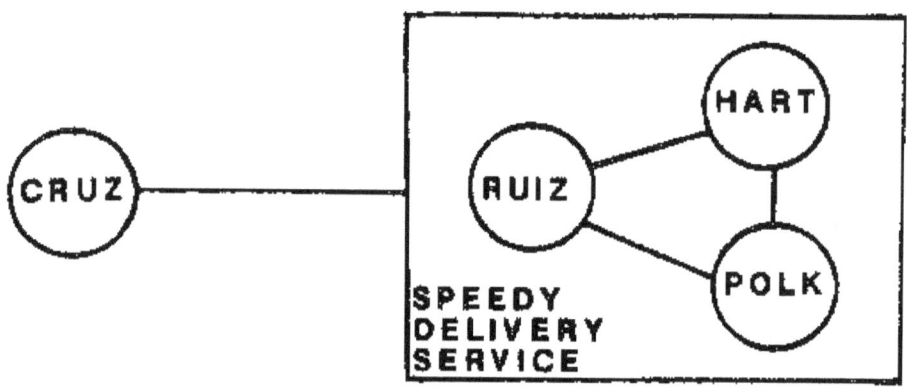

<u>ASSOCIATION BETWEEN ORGANIZATIONS</u>

(INDIVIDUAL LINKS NOT KNOWN)

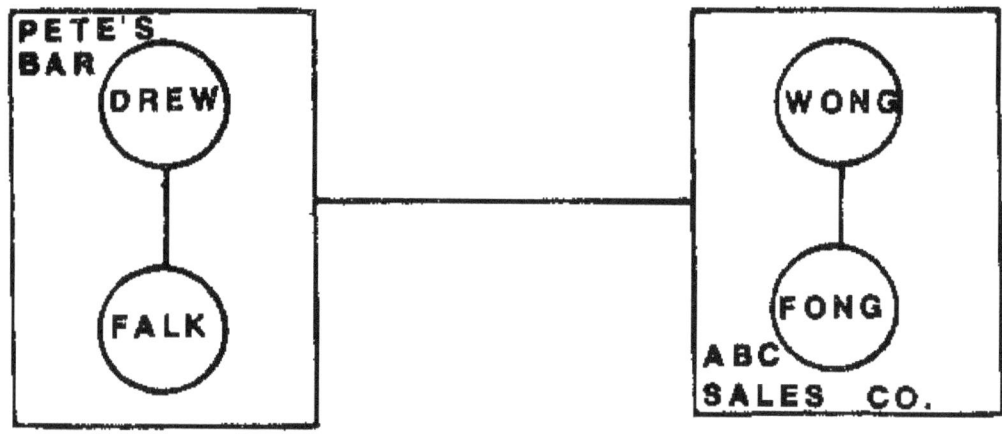

ASSOCIATION BETWEEN KNOWN AND UNKNOWN SUBJECTS

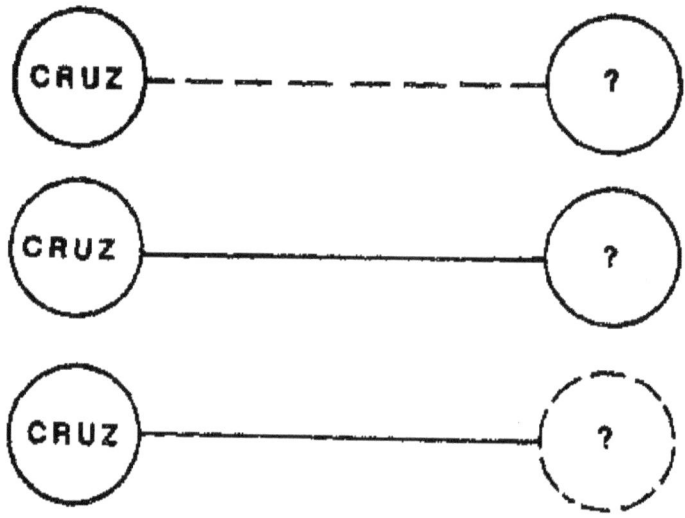

SUBJECTS BEING FORCED OUT OF AN ORGANIZATION

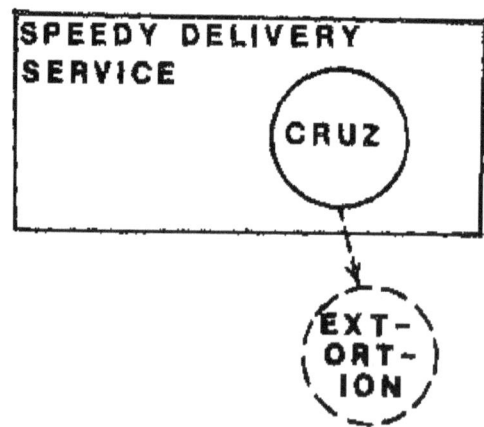

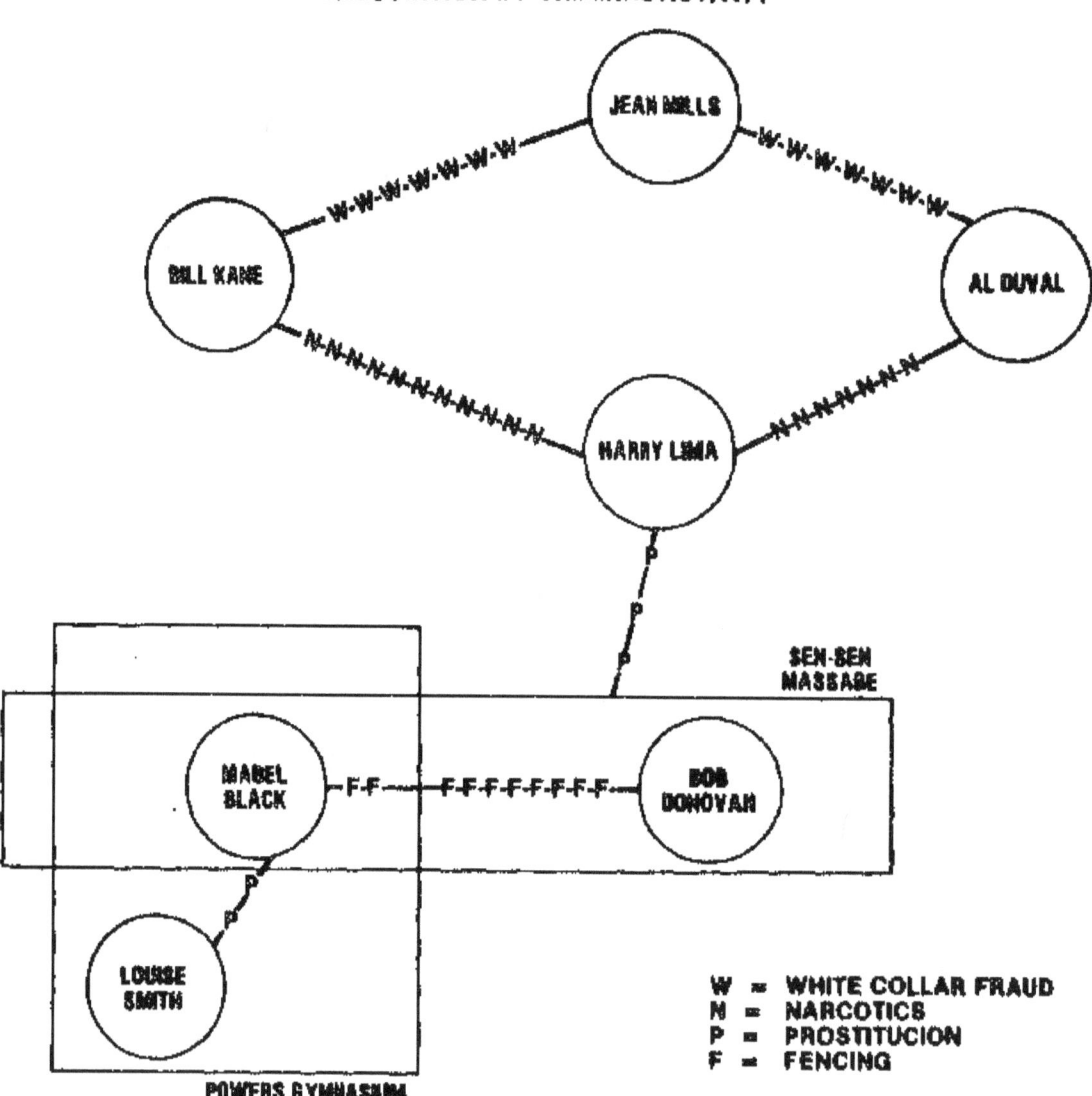

ASSOCIATION BY CRIMINAL ACTIVITY

W = WHITE COLLAR FRAUD
N = NARCOTICS
P = PROSTITUCION
F = FENCING

COMMODITY FLCW

An additional analytical tool that should be seriously considered during informational analysis is the commodity flow. This method helps show the relationships between historical events that relate to goods and services and, the ultimate goal of a criminal network, the receipt of money. As we will see, the commodity flow diagram is closely related to the link diagram and when the two are used in combination, can aid in the clarification of relationships.

COMMODITY FLOW ANALYSIS

Most criminal activities of an organized nature involve the flow of some type of commodity - money, narcotics, arms, stolen goods, etc. Consequently, an understanding of the criminal operation or organization requires an understanding of the flow of commodities involved. For example, tracing the flow of money in a narcotics trafficking network will help to identify key persons who are not directly involved in the flow of drugs. The connecting lines and arrows show the direction of flow. The form of a commodity flow chart is illustrated in the following example.

INFORMATION INPUT

GREEN SELLS OUNCES OF COCAINE TO WHITE AND OTHER STREET VENDORS.

GREEN BUYS A KILO OF COCAINE AT A TIME FROM BLUE, A MAJOR SMUGGLER,
WHO IMPORTS DRUGS BY MEANS OF HIS IMPORT BUSINESS "WORLD TREASURES".

BROWN, A PILOT EMPLOYED BY BLACK DELIVERS MULTIKILOS OF COCAINE FROM BLACK TO BLUE.

BLUE PAYS BLACK BY MEANS OF TRANSFERS OF FUNDS FROM BLUE'S BANK ACCOUNT TO BLACK'S BANK ACCOUNT.
AFTER EACH TRANSACTION WITH GREEN, BLUE TRANSFERS FUNDS FROM HIS BANK ACCOUNT, TO THE BANK ACCOUNT OF ROSE.

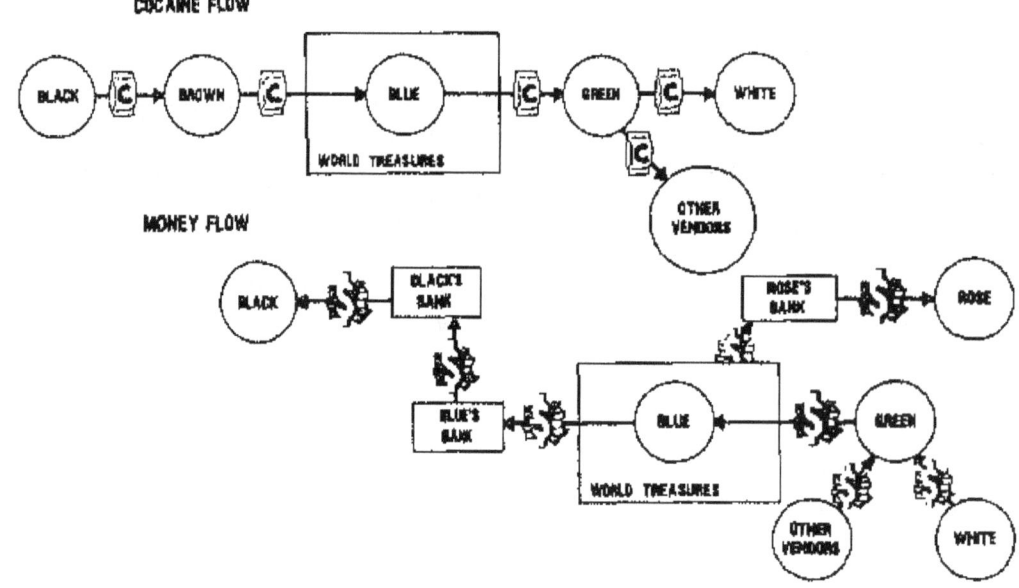

LINK DIAGRAMS FOR TELEPHONE TOLL ANALYSIS

The data listed below represents toll calls made from various phones. Construct a link diagram showing:

a. The interconnecting network of phones by listing number.

b. The stations initiating calls.

c. The frequency of calls to and from each station.

(Assume the data represents a one week period and that all calls are made using the same area code.)

Calls Logged Out From	Numbers Called	Calls Logged Out From	Numbers Called
965-2941	684-2911	843-9299	684-2911
	687-1437		965-2941
	843-9299		684-2911
	684-2911		687-1437
	843-9299		
		687-1437	
684-2911	843-9299		922-0110
	966-6157		922-0110
	687-1437		965-2941
	843-9299	922-0110	(No toll
	965-2941		calls re-
			corded)

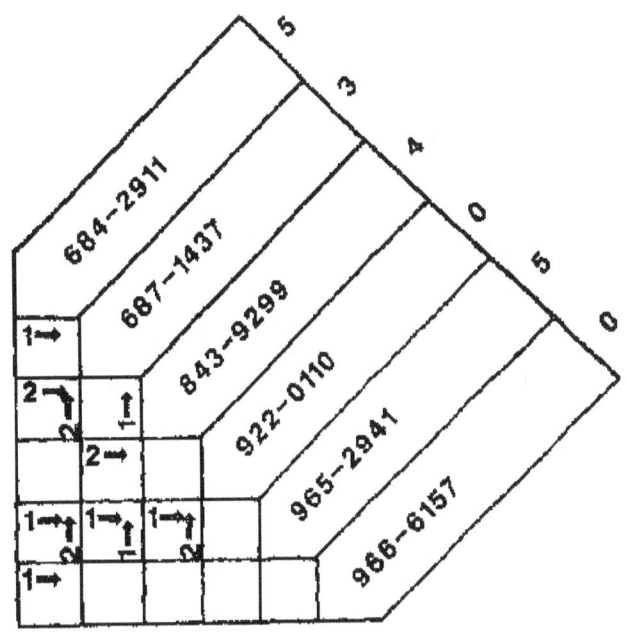

TOTAL STATIONS CALLED FROM 684-2911 = 5
TOTAL STATIONS CALLED FROM 687-1437 = 3
TOTAL STATIONS CALLED FROM 843-9299 = 4
TOTAL STATIONS CALLED FROM 922-0110 = 0
TOTAL STATIONS CALLED FROM 965-2941 = 5
TOTAL STATIONS CALLED FROM 966-6157 = 0

ASSOCIATION MATRIX OF TOLL CALLS

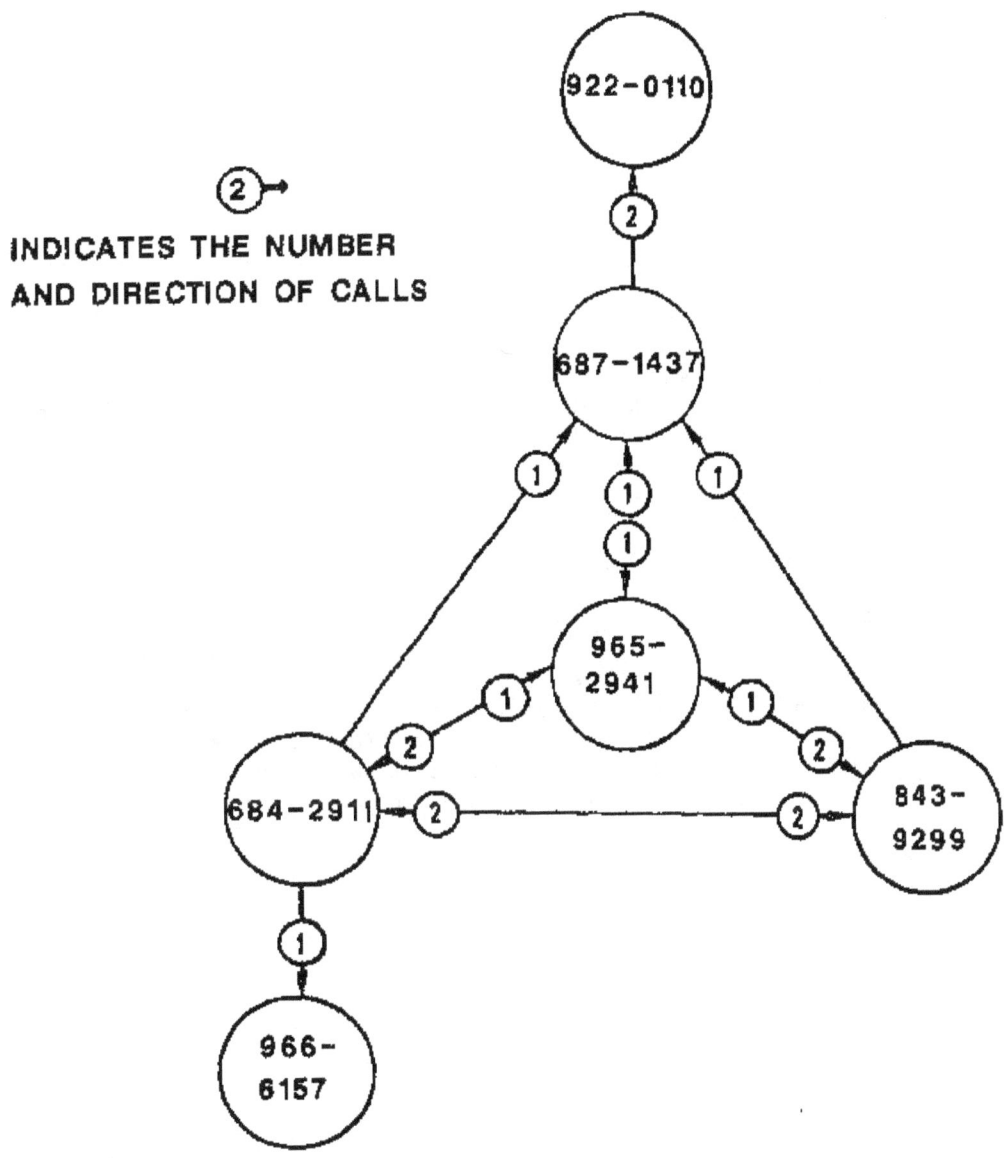

LINK DIAGRAM SHOWING TELEPHONE TRAFFIC BY ORIGINATING STATION WITH FREQUENCY OF CALLS

INVESTIGATIVE ACTIVITY CHARTING

During this session, two additional methods will be presented for the
integration of Information. Whereas link analysis helped you show the
relationships among Individuals and organizations, these methods will help
you show the relationships among events that have happened and analyze
criminal activities; In-class exercises will give you the opportunity to
practice both methods after it has been presented.

EVENT FLOW ANALYSIS

Event flow charts are used to show a sequence of events so the times of
occurrence and relationships among events are clarified. Event flow analysis
is often performed early in the analysis of a complex case to provide a clear
picture of what has happened. The resulting chart consists of brief
descriptions of events enclosed in symbolic areas (circles, rectangles,
etc.)connected by lines. Arrows are employed to show the direction of flow.
The form of an event flow chart is illustrated in the generalized example
shown below.

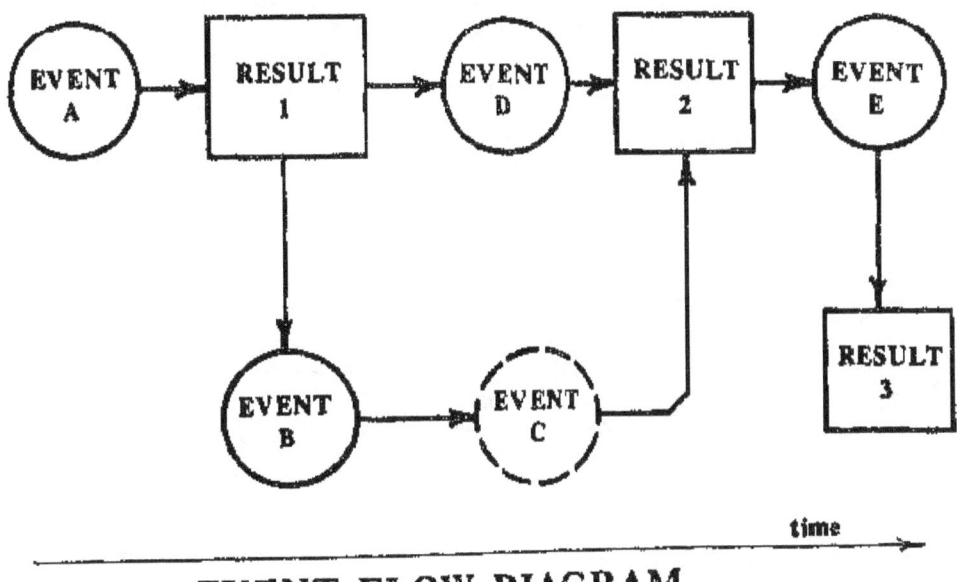

EVENT FLOW DIAGRAM

The significance of the configuration of the symbolic area will depend upon what the investigator or analyst may wish to make of special significance. It is not mandatory that the symbols be different. The same configuration may be utilized throughout the diagram. In the simple example below, the rectangles would represent the establishment of surveillance at specific locales. The circles represent the information derived from an Informant and the surveillance. The broken circle shows an assumed event. Boyd is observed to visit Earth Chemical Supply but is lost by surveillance. He is next observed by surveillance established at Smith's residence and next seen leaving the residence with Smith. We assume Boyd brought the package to the Smith residence unobserved.

Once you have developed a set of symbols, stay with that system. If a different significance 1s attached to one symbol in one investigation and a different significance to the same symbol in another investigation, considerable extra work and confusion could result should the two investigations be found to be related.

You should also note that the elevation of symbols above the "time" line can be of importance to the overall clarity of the diagram. Although it is not always possible, an attempt should be made to have directly related aspects of the investigation along the same elevation. In the example, Boyd and Smith events are at one elevation with another elevation being utilized associated with earth chemical supply.

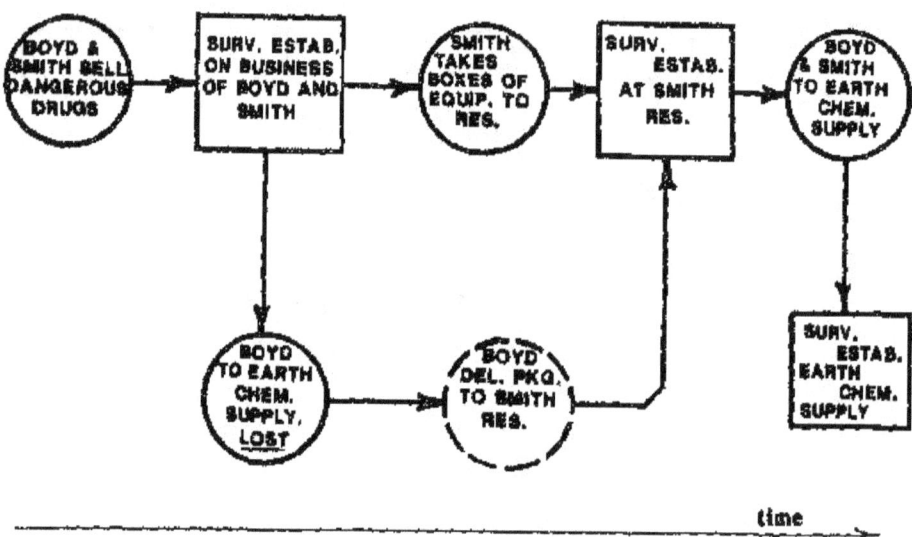

ACTIVITY FLOW CHARTS

Activity flow charts are useful 1n Illustrating a process or sequence of activities directed toward some objectives, where one activity depends upon the completion of another. Much can be learned from such charts about the sequential nature and vulnerability of both organized criminal activities and the law enforcement operations designed to combat them. Activity flow charts are typically of the form shown below.

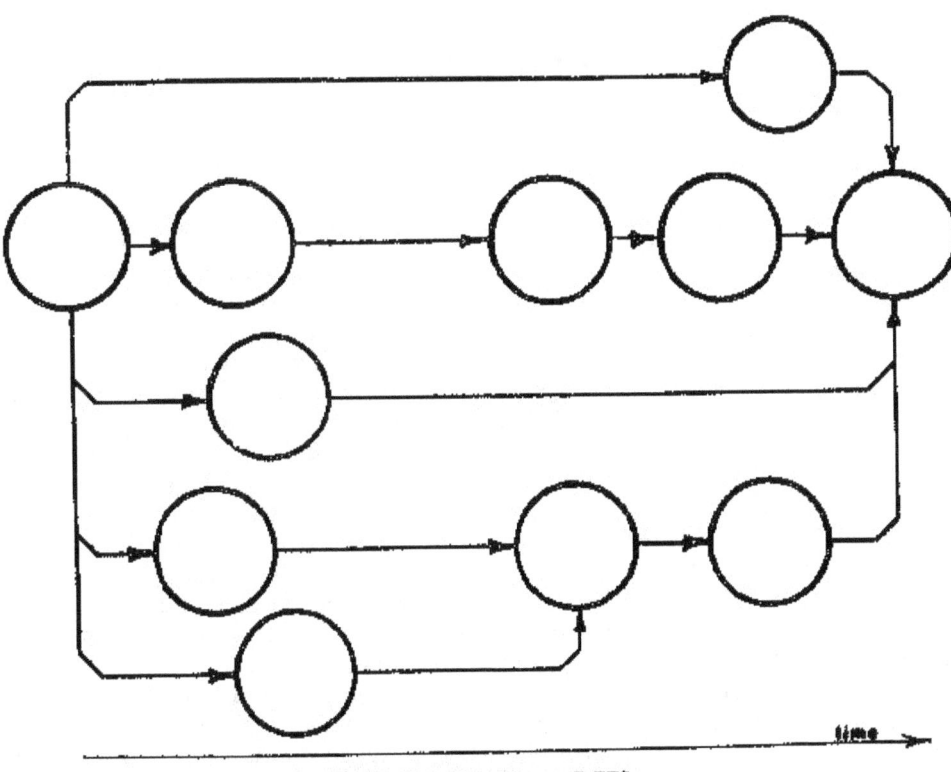

**ACTIVITY FLOW
(CRITICAL PATH)**

5 FINANCIAL INVESTIGATIONS

I. INTRODUCTION

All businesses require assets in order to obtain goods, deliver them to their customers, to promote sales and to grow. A criminal enterprise is no different. The drug trafficker's principal motive is to make a profit from his illicit activities. In order to do so, he requires assets, usually money and property, in order to produce, obtain, and market his goods. The trafficker also needs money to buy silence from witnesses, to pay bribes, expand into other illegal activities, and to move about in order to take advantage of new sources of supply and new markets. He requires funds to entice new prospects into his organization and pay any legal expenses he might incur. Finally, he needs money to support himself in the style which he prefers. In this sense, assets are at the heart of all businesses. As long as assets go untouched, lost workers, products, and their means of transportation can easily and quickly be replaced. Even with the heads of organizations in jail, trusted associates continue the dangerous and deadly business of drug trafficking utilizing the wealth and property left behind. And those imprisoned quickly return to drucr dealing after being released, because criminals making huge profits see* jail as an acceptable risk as long as they don't lose their earnings in the process. They can invest their illegal fortune while in jail, and the money, with interest, will be waiting for them when they get out. There is no need to go through the tedious and risky business of starting all over again.

In recognition of the above, a new and devastating tactic has been developed by narcotics law enforcement. The Drug Enforcement Administration, for example, is implementing a program that strikes at all dimensions of drug trafficking. DEA is continuing to emphasize traditional objectives of arresting major dealers and seizing large amounts of drugs. In addition, however, the financial investigative method has enabled the seizure of the trafficker's ill-gotten gains, and this has proved especially crippling to the criminal. Today's drug enforcement officers can no longer confine themselves to the more traditional aspects of the drug investigative process. During every phase of the investigation they must now ask: "What about the assets and profits?" If we are ever to be successful against drug traffickers, we must identify and locate their assets and confiscate their ill-gotten wealth.

Just what are we talking about when we discuss the assets derived from trafficking? It is estimated that in 1980 the retail street level transaction value of the drug trade in the United States alone was approximately 80 billion dollars. This is a 22% increase from the preceding year, and it is certain that this figure continued to escalate in subsequent years. By way of comparison major corporations in the United States in 1980 ranged from a high of 103 billion dollars (Exxon) to 40 billion dollars (Standard Oil of California) . The drug business ranked second to Exxon in this comparison. It is clear then that the profit motive for the trafficker is powerful and compelling. In the same year, 1980, heroin sales generated over 8 billion dollars from 4 metric tons smuggled into the U.S., 17 billion dollars for dangerous drugs, 30 billion for cocaine and 25 billion for marijuana. It is obvious that such enormous profits make drug trafficking an attractive venture. Traffickers believe it worth the risks inherent in such an illegal enterprise.

In addition to the obvious detrimental effect of the drug traffic on society, the unchecked flow of "narcodollars" can have a much more insidious effect. In many areas of the world where these drugs are cultivated, processed and sold, the influx of these "narcodollars" and the subsequent power it provides can substantially affect the* economic and political climate of the area involved. Both Bolivia and Colombia have fallen victim to this situation in the past as well as many other countries. In consumer nations like the U.S., the "narcodollar" effect on the local community can result in the growth of criminal enterprises. Where the drug traffic prospers, other illegal activities, i.e., prostitution, extortion, theft, etc. also flourish well. In addition, the vast volumes of untaxed dollars generated by the drug traffic help to falsely inflate the prices of certain commodities in the local area. Anyone who has ever tried to purchase a high speed boat or home on a waterway with access to the ocean in the Miami area will see this for himself. The overall result is artificially high prices which damage the local market structure.

II. HISTORICAL PROSPECTIVE

Although the seizure of assets represents a fairly recent strategy in the drug enforcement repertoire, the concept itself is rooted in the ancient forfeiture laws. These laws recognized the inherent right of authorities to confiscate anything used or acquired illegally or which presented a danger to society. In spite of certain historical examples where this right was used to persecute specific groups of people, substantial legitimate precedent exists for the judicious application of -this technique. For example, the power of forfeiture was used by the First Congress of the United States to confiscate pirate, smuggling, and slave ships. Since that time many other forfeiture statutes have been enacted. Every country in the world has forfeiture statutes incorporated within its own legal code although whether or not these laws exist or apply to the drug traffic requires an individual study on each case.

The development of criminal and civil statutes in the area of drug law enforcement is a fairly recent phenomenon in the U.S. and is a result of pressure brought about by the significant drug problem existing in the U.S. Some modification of the law had to be made to assist federal authorities in the war against the traffic and this was, in fact, accomplished with the cooperation of the Congress. With the passage of the Controlled Substances Act in 1970, the first use of the forfeiture power to confiscate the profits and assets of drug traffic was established. Under United States Code 21 USC 848, any individual who is determined to be the leader of a continuing criminal enterprise will, upon conviction, forfeit any profit, interest in, or source of influence over any enterprise obtained through his illegal activities. A close examination will reveal that because the forfeiture of the assets is dependent upon a conviction, the burden of proof is entirely on the government. If the criminal charge should be dismissed of a technicality, reduced to a lesser charge by the judge or prosecutor, or if the defendant is found not guilty, the government cannot proceed with the forfeiture. It was subsequently observed that the difficulty in obtaining convictions under this statute due to the burden of proof frustrated many efforts, on the part of the authorities, to seize traffickers' assets.

Another law which was passed at approximately the same time was the Bank Secrecy Act. This law required all banks and financial institutions to report all transactions over $10,000 to the U.S. Treasury Department. These mandatory reports, including activity in foreign accounts, provided law enforcement with an excellent vehicle for the identification of traffickers' assets. It also provided a means for tracing the flow of narcodollars through the various national and international banking institutions because the law provided the authority to examine bank records with a court order. More will be said about banks, money flow, and other aspects of money maneuvering in a subsequent portion of this manual.

In 1978, the U.S. Congress, responding to a need for a better forfeiture law, passed 21 USC 881 which is a civil statute as opposed to a criminal one. This law provided for the seizure of all assets which were:

(1) Exchanged or offered in exchange for drugs

(2) Proceeds from a narcotics transaction

(3) Any cash or securities used to facilitate any violation of the Controlled Substances Act

The important point to remember is that this act is a civil procedure and is not dependent upon the conviction of the defendant. The dismissal of criminal charges against the owner of the assets seized does not damage or nullify the civil proceeding against the assets. These proceedings are not burdened by the complexities involved in criminal cases. In addition, the burden of proof shifts from the government to the defendant. The government can also introduce more kinds of evidence in civil cases than is permitted in criminal cases which makes a successful outcome easier for the government. The results of this new law have been impressive. In only three years time the* DEA seized 268 million dollars from drug dealers. Other agencies, acting upon information and assistance from DEA seized an additional 154.2 million. Numerous other large asset seizures have subsequently been accomplished.

III. FORFEITURE AS A LAW ENFORCEMENT TECHNIQUE

It takes time - a long time - to enlighten thousands of police officers, prosecutors, judges, and law makers in the necessity and value, of new laws such as those which enable the forfeiture of criminals 1 assets. As the educational process on forfeiture continues, the amount and variety of assets seized should dramatically increase. It is certainly possible that drug enforcement programs could be self-supporting. At that point the cost to governments of these programs will be offset by the fortunes seized from drug dealers. In addition certain assets seized, e.g., vehicles, vessels, and aircraft, could be turned over for immediate use by law enforcement agencies, thereby saving additional operating costs. Ihe financial investigative method will require a joint law enforcement effort between a nation's own domestic agencies, e.g., DFA, FBI, Customs, etc., and international agencies as well, such as INTEKPOL, EPIC, and the various federal authorities of all countries. Through this cooperative effort, traffickers can be targeted, assets identified, and prosecution brought against the financiers and money launderers who generally escape the attention of the authorities. While all countries endeavor to arrest drug dealers and seize illicit drugs, very few are involved in the seizure of drug profits. For too long the motive behind drug trafficking has been ignored. A principal reason is the lack of forfeiture laws or effort to test existing laws. During the 48th Session of the General Assembly of ICPO-INTERPOL in Nairobi in September 1979, a resolution was adopted requesting member countries to make all possible efforts to monitor and suppress financial transactions relating to illegal activities. Several countries, e.g., Switzerland, Jamaica and the Cayman Islands have initiated efforts to make the concealment of drug trafficking profits more difficult. The Policia de Investiqaciones del Peru (PIP) has established a financial investigation group which is dedicated to the identification of traffickers' assets for possible seizure. A main objective of this course is to raise consciousness on the part of all law enforcement authorities to possibilities offered by this technique in the war against the drug traffic.

CONCEALED INCOME ANALYSIS

Financial investigation, as you already know, is a tool that causes devastating financial loss to the criminal. One specific aspect of that technique is known as concealed income analysis or the net worth method. The purpose of net worth analysis is to determine the extent to which a person, group, or organization receives and benefits from money obtained from other than legitimate sources.

The net worth principle has been commonly used by government tax authorities for the purpose of determining taxpayers' income tax liabilities, primarily in those instances where no books or records of income and expenses have been maintained by taxpayers from which a determination of tax liability could be made.

Recently, DBA has implemented the net worth principle to determine the extent to which a person, group, or organization is receiving and benefitting from money obtained from narcotics trafficking. When DBA is able to show evidence of drug trafficking, the courts often accept a presumption of that trafficking as the source of unexplained income.

From that presumption, the courts also recognize the forfeiture of assets which are the product of that unexplained source of income. It is constructive to now define some of the terms and concepts cannon to the net worth analysis procedure.

1.   ASSETS: Something of value, either cash or a commodity which can be converted to cash.

a. Real property (House)

b. Personal property (Automobile)

c. Stocks and bonds

d. Jewelry

e. Furs

2. LIABILITY: A financial obligation involving an oral or written premise to pay.

a. Short-term loan

b. Mortgage

c. Automobile or boat loan

3. NET WORTH: At a specified point in time, total assets minus total liabilities. (What a person owns r less what he owes.)

4. INCOME: Money (or goods) received in return for services (or goods) over a period of time.

a. Salary

b. Profits

c. Interest

5. EXPENSE: Payments for consumables as part of living (or doing business) over a period of time.

a. Food

b. Gasoline

c. Taxes

d. Medical care

e. Travel

f. Entertainment

The specific information pertaining to these terms and concepts is often difficult to obtain due to the trafficker's deliberate attempts to conceal this data. It will require the astute investigator tn employ all his skills to reveal this information. The following are suggested, possible sources of information:

a. Individual records and books

b. Records in public agencies

c. Records in financial institutions

d. Informants

e. Surveillance

Some useful documents often used to extract valuable financial information are credit applications, financial statements, credit profiles, and loan agreements.

As stated earlier, the purpose of concealed income analysis is to determine whether or not a person has unidentified income (and, therefore, possibly illegal sources of income) . Information on assets and liabilities is needed at three points in time, and information on income and expenditures is nopded for the intervening time periods. Increases in net worth can be calculated, estimates of expenses and income can be included, and the estimated amounts of income from unidentified sources can be determined.

Exhibit 4 provides the model for the format of concealed income analysis. Exhibit 5 provides an example of a typical worksheet. This investigative technique can be extremely powerful in illustrating illegitimate income and can serve as the basis for asset seizure.

Exhibit 4

FINANCIAL ANALYSIS FORMAT

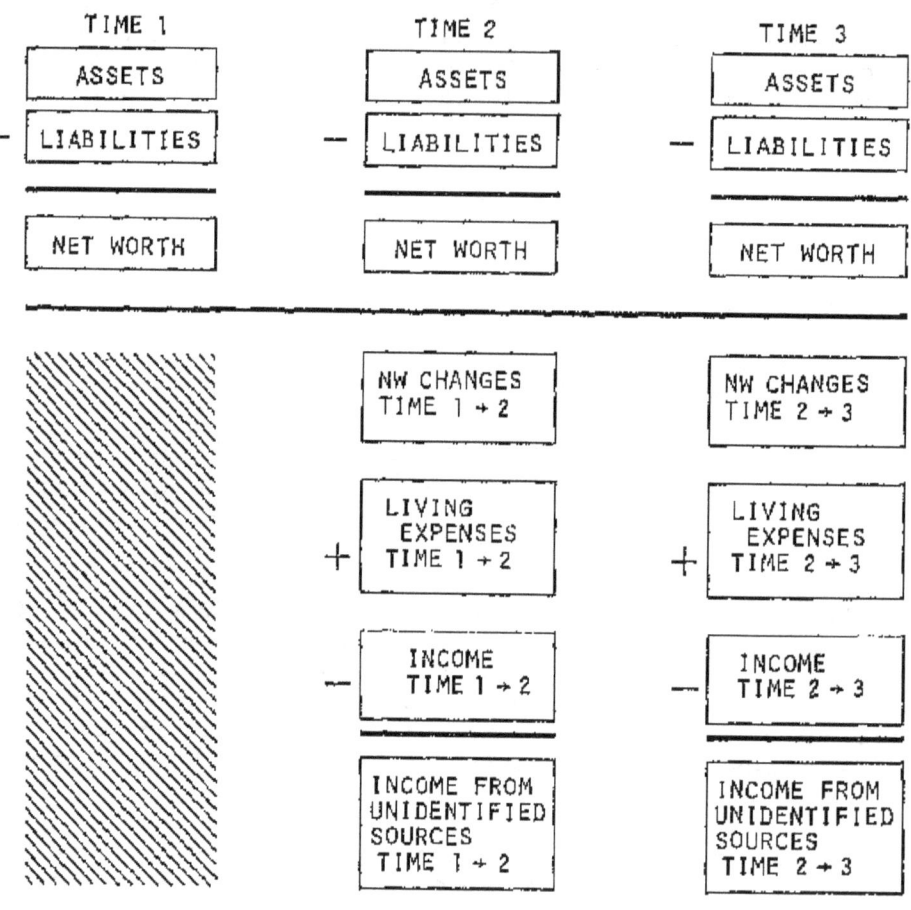

Exhibit 5

FINANCIAL ANALYSIS WORKSHEET FOR
EXAMPLE

ASSETS (+)	12-31-Y1	12-31-Y2	12-31-Y3
Cash in Bank	$ 500	$ 3,000	$ 2,000
Savings Account	10,000	25,000	48,000
House	95,000	95,000	95,000
Stocks and Bonds	10,000	12,000	76,000
Automobiles	7,000	7,000	19,000
TOTAL	122,500	142,000	240,000

LIABILITIES (−)			
House Mortgage	75,000	74,000	73,000
Auto Loan	5,000	3,000	1,000
Personal Bank Loan	10,000	8,000	-0-
TOTAL	90,000	85,000	74,000
NET WORTH	32,500	57,000	166,000
CHANGES IN NET WORTH	/////////	24,500	109,000
TOTAL EXPENSES (+)	/////////	25,000	40,000
TOTAL	/////////	49,500	149,000
INCOME (−)	/////////	30,000	35,000
INCOME FROM UNIDENTIFIED SOURCES		$19,500	$114,000